From:
John

THE LAND OF CARTMEL

THE LAND OF CARTMEL

a History

by

J. C. DICKINSON, M.A., M.Litt., F.S.A., F.R.Hist.S.

(Former Fellow of Emmanuel and Pembroke Colleges, Cambridge; ex-President of the Cumberland and Westmorland Antiquarian and Archaeological Society.)

FIRST PUBLISHED 1980 BY
TITUS WILSON & SON LTD.,
28 HIGHGATE,
KENDAL, CUMBRIA.

© J. C. Dickinson

ISBN 0 900811 12 9

PRINTED BY TITUS WILSON & SON LTD., KENDAL.

PREFACE

The following pages seek to present for the general reader a brief and up-to-date account of the history of the Cartmel area, which will supplement J. Stockdale's massive but costly *Annals of Cartmel* (1872), an invaluable work which, however, inevitably now requires a certain amount of revision. It is much regretted that the inflation of our days has made it advisable to make the book a good deal shorter than is desirable, and because of this to pay only very slight attention to the Cartmel history of the last hundred years, though it must be admitted that this period contains little that is very colourful. There is no doubt that a good deal of the archaeological history of the area still awaits discovery and assessment. Knowledge of the course of Cartmel's history in medieval times is very much more fragmentary than might have been hoped principally because of the almost total loss of the archives of Cartmel priory and of the medieval Archdeacons of Richmond who exercised very considerable power in our region. Much of what is extant is utilised in the *Victoria County History*.

Unpublished records of the Duchy of Lancaster in the Public Record Office contain some useful Cartmel material. For later times the unpublished Cartmel Church Book (which begins in 1597) and the unpublished Cartmel Enclosure Act are both of high value. The connection of our area with the Lake District, and its quite considerable importance in early industrial times, are but two of the major factors behind the existence of a very considerable documentation for the history of Cartmel in the eighteenth and nineteenth centuries that has not yet been fully utilised. If the present work has done anything to stimulate research into the history of a singularly attractive area I shall be glad. In the fifty years which I have worked on this I have acquired a quite considerable amount of interesting unpublished information on it from friends and relations living in Cartmel, notably from Lucy Agnes Butterworth to whose memory I dedicate this work.

J. C. D.

In memory
of
L. A. B.

ACKNOWLEDGEMENTS

The composition of this work has been aided by help for which I am most grateful from various relations, friends and institutions. My brother Bernard has given me various valuable leads and helped me to follow them up; Mr John Rawson has shared with me his incomparable knowledge of local buildings; Mr Arthur Frearson has aided no little my study of local domestic architecture, and Dr P. A. Newton and Mr Dennis King have greatly assisted my survey of Cartmel's medieval stained glass, the latter giving me access to his unique photographs thereof. Mr R. C. Swift has photographed for me various documents and prints, as well as the misericords of Cartmel priory church. Others who have aided my work on particular points are Miss C. M. Fell, Dr D. C. A. Shotter, Mr J. Clarke of Backbarrow, Mr R. J. Donally, Mr Brett Harrison of the Barrow-in-Furness Record Office, Mr J. P. Shields, Librarian of the Barrow-in-Furness Library and his assistant Mr R. Smith, Dr W. Rollinson, Mr P. Bain-Smith and Mrs L. E. H. Perry. Further I am grateful for the aid of Dr H. Wallis of the Map Department of the British Museum, Mr S. K. Ellison of the House of Lords Library, Mr A. Behrens of the Abbot Hall Museum Kendal, Mr Stephen Penny of the Lancaster Museum and Miss E. Gaddes of the Lancaster Library.

Figure 1 is reprinted from *Domesday Book* Cheshire, including Lancashire Cumbria and North Wales (Phillimore edition, edited by John Morris, 1978) by kind permission of the publishers.

For permission to reproduce illustrations of items in their charge I am indebted to the Lancaster Museum, the Map Room and Dept. of Prints and Drawings of the British Museum, the National Portrait Gallery and the Cumberland and Westmorland Antiquarian and Archaeological Society. I am most grateful to Canon E. Rothwell for his meticulous reading of the proofs of this book and to Messrs. Titus Wilson for the skill and speed with which they have produced it.

CONTENTS

	Page
Preface	v
Dedication	vii
Acknowledgments	viii
Contents	ix
List of Illustrations	xi
List of Figures	xii

Part I—History
- One: The Background 1
- Two: The Medieval Monastery 11
- Three: the Priory Church today 29
- Four: Travel 41
- Five: Matters Economic 54

Part II—Places
- Allithwaite 67
- Broughton and Newton 72
- Cark and Holker 75
- Cartmel (Churchtown) 82
- Cartmel Fell 85
- Flookburgh 88
- Grange 91
- Lindale 93

Appendices	97
Bibliography	107
Index	109

LIST OF ILLUSTRATIONS

facing page

PLATE 1	Cartmel Priory Church from the South West (*c.* 1850)	4
PLATE 2	Misericords in Cartmel Priory Church	5
	a. The Trinity Face.	
	b. The Chase.	
	c. The Pelican in her Piety.	
PLATE 3	Stained Glass in Cartmel Priory Church	20
	a. An Archbishop (? St. William of York).	
	b. Rod of Jesse (*detail*).	
	c. Arms of Cartmel Priory.	
PLATE 4	Choir Stalls in Cartmel Priory Church	21
PLATE 5	The Land of Cartmel from the map by William Yates 1786	36
PLATE 6	a. Lancaster Sands – from an etching after David Cox	37
	b. The Ulverston to Lancaster Coach (*c.* 1840).	
PLATE 7	a. Lancaster Sands by J. M. W. Turner	52
	b. Cartmel Fell Church.	
PLATE 8	Cartmel Fell Church	53
	a. The Crucifix.	
	Stained Glass:	
	b. Ordination.	
	c. Mass.	
PLATE 9	(a and b) Stained Glass from Bowness Church	68
	a. Sir William Thornburgh and his wife.	
	b. William, Prior of Cartmel.	
	c. Lindale and Castlehead before the coming of the Railway.	
PLATE 10	a. Christopher Rawlinson, (1677-1733), scholar	68/69
	b. John Wilkinson (1728-1808), iron master.	
PLATE 11	Vanished Chapels	68/69
	a. Lindale.	
	b. Field Broughton.	
	c. Flookburgh, demolished 1776-7.	
	d. Flookburgh Chapel 1777-1900.	
PLATE 12	a. Wraysholme Tower	69
	b. Cark Hall.	
PLATE 13	a. Canon Winder Hall	84
	b. Holker Hall in 1820.	

PLATE 14   a. Title page of Rev. J. Armstrong's prayer book for the parishioners of Cartmel 84/85
           b. Poster – prosecution of poachers.

PLATE 15   a. Certificate of Cartmel Savings Bank 84/85
           b. The Big Mill, Cark.

PLATE 16   a. Notice of house at Grange, 1811 85
           b. Grange in 1850.

LIST OF FIGURES

Page

FIG. 1   *Domesday Book* (Farley edition 1783), references to Cartmel with English translation 9

FIG. 2   Ground Plan of Cartmel Priory Church 28

FIG. 3   East Window of Cartmel Priory Church 38

FIG. 4   Glass, formerly at Wraysholme Tower 70

FIG. 5   Conjectural diagram of the layout of the Priory of Cartmel 83

PART I—HISTORY

CHAPTER ONE

THE BACKGROUND

THE land of Cartmel, whose history is the concern of this book, at an early stage acquired boundaries of which much the greater part was sharply delineated by geography. From the south-east shore of Windermere Lake, they followed the line of the vigorous river Leven to the estuary which bears its name and thence went onward, down the Cartmel coast-line to its southern tip and then northward up to near Grange-over-Sands whence it followed the little river Winster for a while, finally turning abruptly westward to regain Windermere along a little beck. As will be seen its geology is unusual and much more complex than might be expected for so small a district.

In Norman times the area was known as "the barony of Cartmel". Along with the neighbouring land of Furness it formed part of the county of Lancashire from the time of the formation of the latter in the late twelfth century down to 1974, when on All Fools Day it was moved to the new region of South Cumbria. The old county of Lancashire was early divided into local areas termed "hundreds", Cartmel belonging to that of Lonsdale but since, as we shall see, Cartmel and Furness were geographically cut off from the rest of the county, they were collectively termed the Hundred of Lonsdale North of the Sands, or North Lonsdale, our part later on also coming to be known as "the Ancient Parish of Cartmel".[1] The land of Cartmel is dominated by the twin line of fells which run southward down most of its western and eastern sides. The former is separated from the coast by an extensive flattish area much of which has recently become a Government Nature Reserve, whilst the latter has no little uneven land, much of it covered by Grange-over-Sands. The whole area is noted for the mildness of its climate and the exquisite beauty of its scenery.

The marked remoteness of Southern Lakeland, the comparative poverty of most of Cartmel's soil and its almost total lack of mineral resources inevitably gave it down the centuries a very thin and scattered population which mostly lived either in hamlets or villages or in the massive farmhouses which nestle so neatly in the fellsides. In 1801 Cartmel's population numbered a mere 4,007, which had increased to 6,270 by 1901.

Of the history of the area in all the centuries which preceded the foundation of the medieval priory there we know very little indeed, partly because there never was a

---

[1] In the following pages unless otherwise stated the word Cartmel is here used to cover the whole area here described and not merely the village of that name.

great deal to know, partly because no little of the archaeological material on which this knowledge depends has been destroyed or hidden by time, but principally because very little study of the area has yet been effected with the remarkable techniques developed by the archaeologists of today.

It is certain that pre-historic occupation of Cartmel was not intensive, especially in its northern half, but it is by no means without interest. The only one of the various caves in the area to be adequately explored is that at Kirkhead in a cliff below Allithwaite. Here recent excavation did not produce any spectacular finds but showed that the place had been used by man in the so-called Upper Paleolithic Age (c. 10,000 B.C.) and was thus amongst the oldest pre-historic sites in Northern England. (In view of the fact that before the Railway Age the huge majority of travellers to Lancashire North of the Sands came thither by sea, it is not surprising that the earliest pre-historic site and, as we shall see, the earliest Christian site in Cartmel, are found close to each other below Allithwaite, adjoining what was certainly the best anchorage in the area, which the massive crag of Humphrey Head shielded from the prevailing west winds and where there was provided a far better landing ground than that of the mostly muddy coast line of the western side of the peninsula.)

It is quite possible that an interesting site existing on Holker Bank is of pre-historic date, of which the sole major indication today is the curious boulder known from its shape as the "Frog Stone". Stockdale in his indispensable *Annals of Cartmel* (1872) tells us that this was originally part of a stone circle which was largely destroyed when the Enclosure Movement created great need for stone walling. The fact that the ground in the area is very uneven indeed gives some support to this belief, but is much less weighty than that of a note in an unpublished MS of about 1800 which asserts that there existed here "within the memory of many now living, the ruins of a thick wall, exactly circular, formed of loose stones without any mortar or cement . . . only one large stone (more or less broken) now remains and this along with two others stood about 13 yards from the east side of the ring or circle, the circle itself being of about 126 yards in circumference". This structure is more likely to have been used for domestic than religious purposes. (It is worthy of note that what may well be one very old track ran from Kirkhead, up to Boarbank, down past Birkby to the bottom of the valley and thence past this circle on Holker Bank and on to an ancient crossing of the Leven estuary).

There can be no doubt that there existed in our area an unknown number of pre-historic settlements with their turf walls and beehive huts but none of them have yet been scientifically identified. Place-name evidence does, however, provide proof of two such establishments existing certainly in rather later times and possibly in pre-historic times. The older of these two names is that of Walton (which here probably means "the dwelling or hamlet of the Britons"). This place-name now survives only in Walton Hall, a largish farm which, as we shall see, is one of the very few places in Cartmel which is mentioned in Domesday Book. Walton occupies an attractive situation in a sheltered corner of the hills with a small but lively little beck which, from some unknown date, amongst other things provided power for a useful water-mill. On the other side of the valley also on a well-drained hillside is Birkby, a Norse name probably here meaning "the farmstead of the Britons". A number of prehistoric axes and axe hammers of the Neolithic and Bronze Age have been found in Cartmel – largely at its southern end, including a fine early axe of the pointed butt type discovered at Lindale which was recently presented to Lancaster Museum by the writer. Quite numerous are axe-hammers including the thin-butted type known to have been manufactured in quantity at axe-factories in Langdale in the Neolithic period. Most of these have been found in the low land below Flookburgh which down to quite recent times was a coastal area. Amongst them was a huge axe no less than $13\frac{1}{4}''$ long, found on Winder Moor which now languishes in the British Museum. Not many surviving querns (hand-mills) of this period from Cartmel are known.

Roman Rule

The history of South Cumbria in Roman times has only recently attracted much attention from professional archaeologists, but it is certain that a great deal more knowledge of it still awaits discovery. It opened with the famous campaign of Agricola who established a fort in Lancaster, in or about 80 A.D. and then drove on to Carlisle by way of Tebay and Shap and the Eden Valley. It is clear that for much of the subsequent period the Roman authorities were greatly troubled by raiders attacking the Cumberland coastline, against whom by 130 they had constructed a string of coastal forts, together with a major naval base at Ravenglass (c. 125). The great mountains of Central Lakeland were, of course, very scantily inhabited and their natives posed not the slightest military problem.

Of the history of Furness and Cartmel in Roman times there is very little which as yet can safely be said. In view of the fact that trouble in this area came largely from the sea and not from the land it is rather curious that no traces of a major site have been found at the south end of Furness, where in medieval times there existed at Piel what was one of the major ports of north-west England, but there has been no little erosion of the coast in this area so the sands here may have hidden remains which we would gladly see. In his valuable work *The Romans in North West England* Potter suspects "a military presence at one or more points along" the coast of Furness and Cartmel.

So far as Cartmel is concerned the only site which has so far exhibited more than minute indications of the Roman presence is Castlehead. This is dominated by a stout rock which was planted with trees in quite modern times, probably with the aid of earth transported from its base. When in 1795, the famous local iron-master John Wilkinson built for himself the substantial mansion still to be seen near the rock, a number of interesting archaeological finds were made, though unhappily these were not systematically listed for posterity and most if not all of them have disappeared, no few "sold for a trifle to a Jew in Liverpool" according to Stockdale.[2] From what

[2] It is quite possible that coins from Castlehead are immured in the Department of Coins and Medals at the British Museum, but enquiries there produced no useful information of any kind on this matter.

he and another writer record there were apparently about 75 Roman coins and 95 more of the Anglo-Saxon period which suggest a long continuity of occupation here, whilst the word "Castle" in Cumbrian place-names often implies remains of a pre-medieval stone structure.

Unhappily the presence of Wilkinson's house and his reclamation of much land in the area makes scientific investigation of this site a matter of great difficulty and at present we can only make uninformed guesses about the early history of Castlehead. It is however to be noted that its position at the point where until recent times the rivers Leven and Winster joined to meet Morecambe Bay is just where the Romans might have founded some sort of establishment to provide contact by boat between their coastal shipping in the Lancaster-Ravenglass area and their fort at Watercrook, situated a few miles up the river Kent (one would greatly like to know whether in Roman times this river was tidal as far as this fort as it long was in later centuries at least as far as Levens). In this connection it is interesting to note that at nearby Lancaster is a Roman tombstone commemorating *barcarii*, a highly technical word applied to certain boatmen. Could these have been employed on the Kent? Be this as it may, there is no doubt that the Romans were much too shrewd to build major roads across the Cartmel peninsula for then, as later, the infuriating problems created by the local tides (see p. 41) would have rendered them useless for military purposes; a little road running below Flookburgh to Sandgate is traditionally termed Roman, and may well have existed even in pre-historic times, but can have had no great significance. If the Romans used Lake Windermere for transport, as the situation of the fort of Ambleside down on its northern shore suggests, and if, as has been claimed, some of the stone used to build the fort came from south of the Bay, it would be natural to expect that a road led from the foot of the lake to some southern point on the Cartmel coast. Of this not the slightest trace has been found, though a small lane at the top of Lindale Hill is popularly termed "Roman". However there are indications that there was a Roman road, albeit a short one, in the neighbourhood of Eggerslack on the eastern fringe of Grange-over-Sands. Two charters of about the late twelfth century employ a term to describe a road in this area which in the opinion of an eminent etymologist (Prof. Bruce Dickins) must mean "the Broad Street", a term which at this point in time must imply a road of Roman construction. If, as we shall see (see p. 91) it is virtually certain that there was a small harbour providing safe moorings for shipping at this spot, it would be very natural to link it by a road with the nearby establishment at Castlehead.

Of the civilian life of Cartmel in Roman times very little is yet known, though a few odd coins of the period have been found, including one of Domitian at Kirkhead and "a large brass coin of Adrian" at Broughton. Very much more interesting than these is the substantial hoard of Roman coins accidentally discovered by two labourers working near Walton Hall very early in the last century, notice of which was preserved for posterity by that notable Cartmel antiquary William Field who was providentially sitting in a pub in Churchtown when the finders entered in the hope of exchanging some of their finds for liquid refreshment. Baines' *History of*

Plate 1 — Cartmel Priory Church from the South West (c. 1850).

Plate 2 — Cartmel Priory Church Misericords.

a. The Trinity Face.

b. The Chase.

c. The Pelican in her Piety.

Lancashire asserts that these coins numbered 524; they seem largely to have been minted between the middle of the second and the middle of the third centuries. All or most of them passed into the possession of the then Duke of Devonshire, as owner of the land in which they were found, but their present habitat is unknown.

The Angles

Though schoolbooks link the Angles firmly with the Saxons and Jutes, it is certain that the latter two groups of invaders of Britain never came anywhere near the Lake District and that the Angles who reached North Lancashire were not very numerous and arrived very late. They had originally settled across the Pennines where they established the kingdom of Northumbria which had its capital at York and sprawled over most of northern England. Like the railways of Victorian days, they mostly arrived by way of the Aire Gap and, in these parts, again like the railways, made a main centre at the noble town of Lancaster, whose parish church still preserves some stones which they carved. The date of their arrival here has long been in doubt, but it has recently been estimated that these Northumbrians "made sporadic attacks across the Pennines early in the seventh century, but they seem not to have effected the penetration of the Aire Gap until about 650-70" (P. Hunter-Blair).

Such a chronology fits in admirably with the sole early reference to the history of Cartmel before the Norman Conquest. This occurs in a Durham chronicle, written in the twelfth century, but incorporating material of much earlier date, and tells us that Egfrith, King of Northumbria (670-85) gave to the celebrated St Cuthbert "the land called Cartmel with all the Britons in it" and also a place called *Suthgedluit*, which was then put in charge of an abbot (as we know from other evidence that there was an Anglian abbey at Heversham, it seems likely that this is what this latter name denotes). The special mention of Britons (i.e. old Celtic inhabitants) is interesting; can some of them have been refugees who fled across the bay to avoid the Anglian invaders?

The most notable change in Cartmel wrought by the Anglians almost certainly was the erection here of a place of worship, which may have originally been a chapel served with help from Heversham or Lancaster, but which before the Norman Conquest had acquired an endowment and priest of its own, though this is a plausible guess not an established fact. There can be no doubt that this early church was erected below Allithwaite near the cliff which because of this came to be known as Kirkhead (i.e. "the Church headland") and had near it a now vanished pool which a post-Conquest charter terms "Church pool". The chapel itself fell into ruin very long ago; its site being unknown today, though long ago some graves which almost certainly belonged to it were discovered, which inspired J. Briggs to write a far from fascinating "Elegy, written in the chapel-lands (after the manner of Gray)", in the section of his *Poems on various subjects* (1818) entitled (not inaptly) "Pathetic Pieces".

It is very likely that Angles who settled in Cartmel largely came from the south side of the bay, and were fewish in number. As a people they seemed rather fastidious farmers, who tended to settle only in places where the soil was good. In Cartmel they chose mostly sites in the Ay valley. One of the earliest settlers was probably a certain Hunfrith who gave his name to Humphrey Head. Others pushed northward to found the "new settlement" which we call Newton, a hamlet at the point where the road running north through the land of Cartmel met the track which came up the fell from Westmorland to go on to Furness. A major estate of Anglian origin was Broughton – "the settlement by the brook" – a name which probably originally applied to the place later known as Hampsfield. In later times this was the sole major estate that did not belong to Cartmel priory and in earlier days had probably been the residence of the royal steward in charge of Cartmel. It is one of the very few places in our area with a major pond and a vigorous brook which gave a really good water supply.

The Vikings

The total number of Cartmel place-names of Anglian origin are few, and there is not the slightest doubt that much the most influential of the waves of invasion which affected the history of southern Lakeland was that of the Vikings, which endowed the area with a very high proportion of its place-names and dominated its now sadly undermined dialect. Research has shown very clearly that in South Cumbria these invaders were predominantly of Norwegian origin and, not surprisingly, came mostly not direct from Scandinavia but from the much more accessible lands of Ireland and the Isle of Man. The invasions were very far from being highly organized occurring sporadically and being of varying size. They effectively began in our area in the very first few years of the tenth century, leading the then abbot of Heversham amongst others to retire from the district.

In our part of Lakeland, as elsewhere in much of it the names of Vikings are still with us. Windermere takes its name from one Vinnunder, Thorpensty from Thorfirnr, Allithwaite possibly from Eilifr, Hampsfell from Hamr, Thurston Water (nowadays improperly termed Coniston Lake) from one Thursteinn, Raven Winder from one Hrafn. Amongst the Scandinavian place-names of Lakeland, much more common than those with such personal elements, are others which incorporate certain geographical terms, of which two are very prominent. "*Holme*" in Old Norse means "an isle", "a small island, a water-meadow" and in our area is found in Wraysholme, Rougholme, Waytholme ("an island where hunting is carried on") and also gives its name to the islet near Grange station. "*Thwaite*" is very common in north-western England and is now thought to mean usually "a clearing in woodland, probably used as meadowland, a meadow, a paddock or close". In the Cartmel region we have Allithwaite, Outerthwaite ("the outer thwaite"), Haverthwaite ("the oats thwaite"), Honeythwaite ("the useless thwaite"), Rosthwaite ("the horse thwaite") and Burblethwaite.

Though the Vikings were far from being highly literate they evolved an alphabet of their own composed of Runes. It is of no little interest that this remained in use in South Cumbria no little while after it had fallen into disuse in all or most of the rest of England. At Pennington Church near Ulverston a Runic inscription is still to be seen round the tympanum over its main door, whilst excavations at Conishead Priory revealed a thirteenth-century stone with a personal name inscribed on it in Runic letters. Our local dialect was predominantly Scandinavian, such phrases "Tha mun ga yam, the mother's laitin thee" ("You must go home, your mother is looking for you") "wha's lakin?" (who is playing?) being commonly used by well-instructed locals in the present writer's boyhood. A collection of technical terms used by Flookburgh fishermen carefully compiled by Canon S. Taylor proved to have very close affinities in Icelandic, a finding confirmed in World War II when a Flookburgh man drafted to Iceland found comparatively little difficulty in understanding the local tongue.

By the time of the Norman Conquest of 1066, the land of Cartmel was still far from heavily populated. The village of Cartmel did not exist, nor did that of Cark whilst Flookburgh was little more than a scanty collection of unimpressive fishermens' huts. Newton and Lindale were barely hamlets and Grange-over-Sands almost totally devoid of any inhabitants. The major social element was constituted by the farm-houses most nestling in the hillsides near the not over plenteous sources of fresh water. Then, as in later times, the climate forbade the production of much corn but permitted quite extensive production of oats, from which local bread was, for centuries, extensively made. The local sheep were scraggy-looking but fed contentedly on the not very appetizing fell-sides and produced wool that could be spun into cloth of considerable warmth and durability, whilst cattle-farming was common enough. Apart from Lancaster there was no sizable town to be found for many miles around. Facilities for acquiring even elementary knowledge of reading and writing must have been very scanty indeed, and the fruitful life of monasticism must have been largely unknown. Largely for financial reasons, there were very few parish churches in South Cumbria. Where these existed they mostly served the needs of very wide areas and the place where they were situated was often dignified with the addition to its title of Kirkby – "Church town". Kirkby Stephen, Kirkby Lonsdale and Kirkby Ireleth are titles still with us but those of Kirkby Kendal and Kirkby Cartmel are now no more. "Cartmel" probably means "sandbank by rocky ground" and originally applied to the Grange area.

The Normans

As with most localities, the documentation concerning the early history of Cartmel in pre-Norman centuries is very minute indeed, and even the illustrious *Domesday Book* of 1086 gives us only a few flickers of light on the history of our land. When it was compiled, strange though it may seem, our area and much more of Lancashire was surveyed under the heading of Yorkshire, the name then given to the remains of the ancient kingdom of Northumbria with its capital at York, which at this time covered a huge part of northern England. In these parts, unlike southern areas of the country, the counties with which we are familiar had not yet come into being. *Domesday Book* did not include more than a small fraction of the future

Cumberland and Westmorland, the sole parts of these mentioned therein being the extreme southern tip of the former (around Millom) and a limited area of what was to become southern Westmorland. All of Lancashire North of the Sands was included, albeit in somewhat cursory fashion. Cartmel was not noted as a single unit. We have certain mention of three places here, two of which belonged to the great northern landowner Earl Tostig. These two were Newton (spelt *Neutun*) of which we are told that here the Earl had land assessed at 6 carucates of land and Walton (*Walletun*) where he held the same amount. The third estate recorded is spelt *Cherchebi* which is in effect "Kerkebi" or Kirkby, that is to say "Churchtown" and this must refer to the Anglo-Saxon hamlet in the Kirkhead area where, as we have seen, there was a little church, where, it is noted, "Duan had 6 carucates to geld". It has credibly been suggested that two names recorded in the Book as being in the Craven area are in fact the Holker and Birkby in Cartmel. (Fig. 1).

The whole of North Lonsdale passed into the hands of the Norman kings and became part of the great Honor of Lancaster. The English monarchy had a long and difficult task to maintain control of north-western England. William the Conqueror left us to our own devices, but in 1092 his son, William Rufus, drove up the Eden Valley to Carlisle to seize and fortify the then much-decayed city, a move which his younger brother Henry I sought to consolidate in various ways including the foundation of a diocese of Carlisle (1122-33). In the middle of the century the solid Scots fought back, even briefly pushing down their frontier as far as Preston. However, the English were more numerous, richer and more sophisticated than their northern neighbours (of whom they invariably spoke of in terms of disgust) and as time wore on it became clear that the English frontier would be definitively established along the Carlisle-Newcastle axis, though this by no means prevented the Scots from launching raids over the Border from time to time, a very special trial to which Northern England was to remain subject right down to the Union of England and Scotland in the early seventeenth century.

Some time passed before north-western England was finally divided into the medieval counties which were destined to live so long. The process by which this was effected is a complex one which demands fuller study than it has yet been accorded, but it would seem that by the end of the reign of Henry II (1154-89) that Cumberland, Westmorland and Lancashire had assumed their classic form, the existence of the county of Lancashire being discernible by 1167. Many have wondered why Cartmel and Furness were made part of this latter county instead of being allotted to Westmorland as, at first sight, might seem to have been more reasonable. Medieval bureaucrats had usually a great sense of reality and under the conditions of the time, and indeed for long after, theirs was a perfectly reasonable step, for as we shall see (see pp. 41-4) geography naturally linked Cartmel and Furness with Lancaster. At some uncertain but early date medieval Lancashire was given administrative sub-divisions which were called "hundreds" or "wapentakes". The northernmost of these centred round the Lune and hence came to be called Lonsdale or Lunesdale. Hence, as we have seen, Cartmel and Furness both of which

ⓂIn HOVGVN. h̄b comes Tosti. iiii. car tre ad gld.
In Chiluestreuic. Sourebi. Hietun. Daltune. Warte. Neutun. Walletun. Suntun. Fordebodele. Rosse. Hert. Lies. alia Lies. Glassertun. Steintun. Cliuertun. Ouregraue. Meretun. Penni getun. Gerleuuorde. Borch. Berretfeige. Witinghā. Bodele. Santacherche. Hougenai. Oms̄ hæ uillæ iacent ad Hougun.

ⓂIn Cherchebi. Duuan. vi. car ad gld.
ⓂIn Aldinghā. Ernulf. vi. car ad gld.
ⓂIn Vlurestun. Turulf. vi. car ad gld.
In Bodeltun. vi. car. In Dene. i. car.

327 c
Ⓜ
7 B. In HOLECHER 7 Bretebi h̄b Orm. viii. car træ ad gld.

Y7
M. In **MILLOM** [C] Earl Tosti had 4 c., of land taxable.
In KILLERWICK 3 c., SOWERBY 3 c., HEATON 4 c., DALTON 2 c., WART 2 c., NEWTON 6 c., WALTON 6 c., *SUNTUN* 2 c., FORDBOOTLE 2 c., ROOSE 6 c., HART 2 c., LEECE 6 c., another LEECE 6 c., GLEASTON 2 c., STAINTON 2 c., CRIVELTON 4 c., ORGRAVE 3 c., MARTIN 4 c., PENNINGTON 2 c., KIRKBY IRELETH 2c., BROUGHTON 6 c., BARDSEA 4 c., WHICHAM [W] 4 c., BOOTLE [C] 4 c., KIRKSANTON [C] 1 c., MILLOM (Castle?) [C] 6 c.
All these villages belong to Millom.

Y9
M. In 'KIRKBY' (Cartmel), Dwan, 6 c., of land taxable.
M. In ALDINGHAM, Arnult, 6 c., of taxable.
M. In ULVERSTON, Thorulf, 6 c., taxable.
In BOLTON, 6 c. In DENDRON, 1 c.

Y10
M.
& B. In **HOLKER** and **BIRKBY** Orm has 8 c., of land taxable.   327 c

FIG. 1   *Domesday Book* (Farley edition 1783), references to Cartmel with English translation.

it included, came to be entitled "Lonsdale Hundred North of the Sands" or "North Lonsdale".

There is no doubt that by the close of the twelfth century in North Lancashire as mostly elsewhere in England, population and prosperity had for some time been steadily increasing. In our area the major causes of this were the great social and economic advances which followed in the wake of the foundation of the three monasteries which dominated this area for the rest of the Middle Ages. Of these much the greatest – indeed one of the most important in northern England – was the abbey of Furness, which after being begun at Tulketh near Preston in 1124, moved to what was to be its permanent site, not far from Dalton in 1127. At a very early date it systematically developed the iron deposits in the Lindal area, previously known but little used. Very important economically was Furness' interest in the now increasingly profitable wool trade which led to its acquisition of great tracts of land in Lakeland and on the Pennines for the use of hundreds of sheep. At Piel its early castle stood guard by what soon became the only major port in the region. Much smaller was the priory of Conishead which originated some sixty years after Furness Abbey as a hospital (a term which had a wider sense in medieval times than it now possesses). It was built at the western side of the route that crossed the Leven Sands and must have provided invaluable shelter there to travellers of every kind, even after it was converted into a small priory.

About the end of the year 1185, King John gave "the land of Cartmel" to William Marshal, one of the most illustrious barons in his realm, who by sheer merit had worked his way from very humble origins, to become one of the most prominent and respected nobles of the day in the huge Anglo-French kingdom. In 1189 William acquired through an advantageous marriage, the title of Earl of Pembroke. Very shortly afterwards and just possibly in gratitude for this (though his motives are uncertain), William donated this land for the foundation of a priory at Cartmel – a major new epoch in its history had begun.

CHAPTER TWO

THE MEDIEVAL MONASTERY

OF the church life of the land of Cartmel before the foundation there of its magnificent priory, we know very little, though, as we have seen a small place of worship, perhaps served from the rather short-lived Anglian monastery of Heversham, was established at Kirkhead. Of its later history we know nothing, apart from a few references to its parsons here in the twelfth century. It is quite possible that here, as was not infrequent in northern parts by Norman times, the endowment of the church had become in fact a hereditary estate held by married clergy. If, as is possible, the church itself had become ruinous in Viking times, it may well have been restored in post-Conquest times. The position of Kirkhead at the extreme southern tip of the Cartmel area clearly made attendance at the church there a major undertaking for those living in the Cartmel Fell area, though there the population was certainly very small.

The Foundation of the Priory

The foundation of a medieval monastery was usually a complex process which engrossed some little time, and this was certainly the case here. Probably late in 1190 the future King John as Lord of the Honor of Lancaster, issued a charter confirming "that William Marshal may establish a monastery of any order he likes in the land of Cartmel". But previously, probably early in 1190 and quite certainly not before 1189, William's foundation charter for his priory appeared, its text being preserved for us in a confirmation of Edward II. The document bristles with legal technicalities but its main provisions are that the house was to be one of regular canons, was to have the land of Cartmel with all its appurtenances including iron mines, was never to be made an abbey, was to be independent of any other house, and have its head chosen by the founder or his legal successor from two candidates proposed by the convent (see App. I). From other and later documents we learn that the spiritual charge of the parishioners was to be in the hands of a secular priest appointed and removable by the convent, and that the first inmates of the priory were drawn from the priory of Bradenstoke in Wiltshire. The number of these brethren is quite uncertain, but it was very usual at this time to have a prior and twelve brethren (symbolic of Christ and the twelve apostles) and this may have been the case here.

The technical title of the brethren who were established in the priory was "regular canons of St Augustine", but in popular English usage this cumbrous title was replaced by that of "black canons", (from the colour of the cloaks which brethren wore over their habit when outside). Their order originated obscurely and rather haphazardly largely in central Italy and southern France, getting official approval at the Lateran Councils of 1059 and 1063. Though no few of their communities were established in existing churches, sometimes large colleges or cathedrals, others grew in minor places and even on remote deserted sites. Although their title suggests that "Austin canons" (as English folk termed them) were clergy engaged in pastoral work this was by no means always the case and it is now clear that even those of their members who were in priests' orders did not usually labour in parishes, partly because this could not be combined with the considerable claims of their conventual life, which was on elaborate and conservative lines, not differing much from that of Benedictines. Its primary concern was the perpetual offering of a complex round of daily worship by the whole community. This opened in the earliest hours of the day with a very elaborate office of Mattins which was followed at intervals by six other similar but shorter offices and by a conventual mass as well as a certain number of private masses. The so-called *Rule of St Augustine* which they had adopted was far from being an elaborate guide to their daily life, consisting of a short series of brief injunctions; it was therefore augmented by no few "observances" which regulated their whole complex way of life and were to some degree nurtured by the experience of the Benedictines, though being rather less exacting on certain points. The grounds of their monasteries were usually quite spacious, enclosed by a great precinct wall and entered by a usually elaborate gatehouse, and were not to be left by the canons without some special reason.

General History

The internal history of medieval monasteries, like that of modern clergy-houses was very largely uneventful. At first there was some minor trouble at Cartmel over the mode of election of the priors of the house, and towards the middle of the thirteenth century some internal dissension amongst the brethren was serious enough to be referred to Rome. In these days North Lonsdale was in the mighty diocese of York (which included not only all Yorkshire but half the Lake Counties) so Cartmel priory was liable to periodic visitation by the archbishops of this diocese, though these dignitaries were very over-worked and scarcely ever found it desirable to undertake the long and difficult journey to Cumbria. Only one of the reports of such a visitation is known to have survived – that made by archbishop Wickwane whose tiring journey brought him to Cartmel in 1281. Here he found no major iniquity but several comparatively minor matters in need of correction.

After the very detailed and careful enquiry usual on such an occasion, he issued a number of injunctions aimed at correcting what was amiss. Brethren were to observe strictly the rules regarding silence in the monastery and not allow secular or base people to enter the infirmary, refectory or cloister. Talking with women in church during the cloister procession or elsewhere, was strictly forbidden without the permission and presence of the prior. The observances which complemented *the Rule of St Augustine* were to be firmly observed. Donations made for the building fund were not to be used otherwise. The cloister doors were to be kept shut and priests were to celebrate with pure consciences. Those of the brethren who had acquired for their private use, saddles and other necessities for riding, were to give them to the prior for issue as occasion required. The canons were not to go outside, especially to engage in hunting, without the permission of the prior or the presiding brother. No-one was to be given an office for reasons of kinship, but only on merit, and those who had been professed were to obey the prior. These injunctions mostly follow the stock pattern of such things at this time and do not suggest the existence of anything more than a certain slackness. After this period we have very little evidence regarding the internal life of the priory, and probably largely it is a case of "no news is good news".

Very long afterwards, in 1390, a papal mandate to the archbishop of York ordered the latter to investigate accusations that the prior of Cartmel, William, had been guilty of dilapidation, of simony in admitting canons to profession and of too frequent visits to taverns, so that the buildings of the monastery were falling into ruin; divine worship and hospitality were neglected and scandal caused by the prior's unworthy life. Medieval complaints of this type were often over lurid and as the prior was not removed from office, it is very likely that his lapses were much less serious than they were asserted to be. Almost certainly, as we shall see, ruinous buildings were present in his time, but largely owed their condition to causes outside his control. Probably one good effect of the enquiry may well have been the commencement of an elaborate and much needed restoration of the priory church and cloister (see p. 19).

In this remote part of England secular events of more than trivial interest were rare in the extreme. Very violent and unexpected were the brutish Scottish raids of 1316 and 1322 which wrought immense damage in the area, notably to its slender supplies of crops and stock. As the *Lanercost Chronicle* informs us, in the latter year the Scots "went beyond the Leven sands to Kertemel and burnt the lands around the priory of black canons and took away cattle and booty". So enormous was the damage wrought to the region at this time that royal officials, by no means given to generosity, greatly reduced assessments of ecclesiastical wealth in the area, that of the rectory of Cartmel falling from £46. 13s. 4d. to £8.

A century and a half later, there occurred nearby a spectacular event in Cartmel history – the passage of a massive army which had landed at Piel on 4 June 1487. The Parliament Rolls quaintly noted now the arrival of "a great navie in Furnes in Lancashire . . . accompanyed with a great multytude of stranngers with force and armes, that ys to saye, swerdys, speris, marespikes, bowes, gounes, harneys, brigandynes, hawberkes and many other wepyns and harnes defencible". This massive array, undoubtedly the most imposing assembly the port of Piel ever witnessed, was nothing less than an invasion force which aimed to overthrow the reigning King of England, Henry VII, and replace him by its leader, one Lambert Simnel, who purported to be Edward, Earl of Warwick and had just been crowned as Edward VI in Dublin, but was in fact very much a social nobody. The force would follow the old route across the Leven and Kent sands passing through Flookburgh, and it got as far as Stoke on Trent. Here it was engaged and totally defeated by a royal army, Lambert being captured; instead of decapitating him the noble King found him a post of scullion whence he later rose to be falconer.

There had been a certain amount of local support for the rebels, notably from Sir Thomas Broughton of Broughton-in-Furness who, after the defeat of his side, is said to have died in hiding and to have been buried in Witherslack woods. Such folk inevitably involved their followers in what was without doubt treasonable behaviour and here the local situation was thought serious enough for King Henry to obtain from the pope an official condemnation of such traitors who were declared "to be accursed with the great curse and from the sight of Almighty God and the holy company in Heaven, to be cast out and departed to everlasting damned company...". This precept the king ordered the abbot of Furness and prior of Cartmel to read out publicly in their churches "wherein ye shall singlerly please us".

In 1535 came a heraldic visitation in which was officially recorded the coat of arms of Cartmel priory, which was described as *Party per pale or and vert, a lion, rampant gules*, which in unofficial terms means a shield divided vertically into gold and green halves with a red lion rampant superimposed on them, a good medieval representation of which is preserved in the glass of the middle window in the south wall of the Town Choir of Cartmel priory (Pl. 3c).

Possessions

What properties did Cartmel priory own? To this question the very scanty evidence which has been published does not allow us to give the very detailed answer feasible in the case of the neighbouring abbey of Furness, which has left us copies of literally hundreds of its charters that are all in print. However it is clear that the possessions were very far from massive, though enough to support a community of modest size such as was Cartmel priory. A charter of John of 1199 gives us invaluable particulars of the house's earliest acquisitions – the land of Humphrey Head, given by Gilbert of Bolton (le Sands), part of the pool called "Kirkepol" (i.e. Churchpool), probably near Kirkhead, an acre of land in Humphrey Head which Simon, son of Uckman, had given and which he held from Gilbert. Also confirmed was a small gift of land in "Melsonebi" (wherever that was) by Gilbert, son of Ivo and two acres of land in "Estref holm", another unknown place, but perhaps near Wraysholme. Alan, son of Ketel, gave more land in Bolton (le Sands) with pasture for eight stock and two horses there, a donation which was probably used by the priory for the small hostel which we know that it later had in this place, doubtless mainly used in connection with the Sands crossing. The priory also acquired half of Silverdale, by gift from Henry de Redmaine and the concession of the prioress and convent of Farewell. Henry also gave the brethren such fishing rights as they needed in the lake of "Haverswater" with saltpans and iron mines, should they be found in the area. Another charter of John, later in his reign, extends royal protection to the prior and canons with all their tenants and possessions in Ireland and allowed them to purchase freely, things needed for their use "throughout all our land of Ireland", where William Marshall had given them the village of Kilrush, the church of Ballysax and chapel of Ballymaden, all in County Kildare. A little later, a useful papal bull of 1233 shows us that at Kilrush the priory had then established a small cell (or small daughterhouse). By now the priory had land in Hest and Newton and an annual pension of two silver marks from the church of Whittington. The priory was early involved in a complex dispute with their neighbour on its southern bank, the lord of the manor of Beetham, over fishing rights in the Kent estuary, which the two parties shared. It could also take fish in the little tarn of Helton. Another charter shows Cartmel priory binding itself to pay a rent of 7s. to the hospital of St John of Jerusalem for "Callan" wherever that was. But the sum total of its revenues was certainly very far from considerable. An indulgence of twenty days to penitents who gave alms for the building of the church of St Mary at Cartmel which the archbishop of York issued at Lancaster in 1230 states that the canons' possessions were so scanty that they could barely fulfil the obligations of hospitality. Six years earlier letters of protection of Henry III hint that the house was in low water, financially.

In 1280 King Edward I licensed the brethren to buy necessaries for their use in Ireland and similar licences appear in the following decades. A harbour whence the prior or his representative sailed for Ireland is mentioned in one document. Its location is not mentioned but Grange is much the most likely place. It probably consisted of little more than a jetty with a barn and building or two nearby.

At the end of the century, in 1291, a great valuation of the wealth of the English church was compiled – the *Taxation of Pope Nicholas*. In this the rectory of Cartmel was valued at the quite high sum of £46. 13s. 4d. Note was taken of an annual pension of £1. 6s. 8d. from the church of Whittington. In 1341 the priory acquired a carucate of land in Holker and six years later more property in Broughton and nearby. After this time little information on the priory's estates is yet known, until the great survey of English ecclesiastical revenue made in 1535, the so-called *Valor Ecclesiasticus*.

Unhappily the information regarding some north Lancashire houses including Cartmel which this mighty compilation gives is less full than might have been desired but nevertheless preserves for us some useful details. The site of the priory with its gardens, orchards, arable land and pasture was valued at £8. 16s. 8d. rents and similar income in the Cartmel area at £60. 4s. 0d. the rent of a water corn mill (almost certainly that at Aynsome) at £6. 0s. 0d. lands in Silverdale, Bolton (le Sands) and Hest (bank) at a mere 78s. The tithes of the rectory brought in £23. 10s. 0d. and the pension from Whittington 53s. 4d. Amongst expenses legally due were a pension of 27s. 8d. due to Conishead Priory and 40s. to two lay clerks serving Cartmel's parish altar, who would probably also get board and lodging from the priory and could augment their income from other sources. Wages to lay officials included one to the bailiff at Silverdale and the largish one of £6 to William Gate "bailiff and conductor of all the lord king's people over the sands of the sea called Cartmel sands". There were also alms to be paid out to "various boys and others" and to seven poor people who prayed daily for the soul of the founder of the priory.

This brief survey estimated the net annual revenue of the priory at £91. 6s. 3d. which put it at the poorer end of the list of English monasteries at this time, though by no means the bottom of the list. Justifiably a protest over its inaccuracy came from the priory.

Of the size of the convent before its fall we have a few particulars which suggest that, as might be expected, it was rather variable. In 1381 there were seven brethren, but at this time, owing to the ravages of the Black Death not long before, probably Cartmel, like most English monasteries had appreciably fewer brethren than was normal. In 1536, on the eve of the dissolution of the priory, there were ten canons, as we shall see. Before this we have an interesting and most unusual glimpse of some brethren of the house who are pictured on a panel of stained glass in Bowness parish church, formerly at Cartmel. These are Thomas Hogson, Willym Baraye, William Purfoot, Roger Thwaites, George Fis... (their names no longer all clear on the glass, but are preserved in a seventeenth-century manuscript). The panel is probably of mid-fifteenth century date.

Cartmel priory was unusual in not owning the right of presentation to any outlying livings, but had the right to serve the parish altar in their great church either by their own brethren or by hired secular clergy; all the known evidence suggests that its charge was mostly given to the latter, who were probably lodged in Priest Lane and gave their name to the well there to be found. The responsibilities of the monastery were much increased by the necessity of maintaining considerable farming activity and by involvement in various forms of social aid, notably the dispensation of hospitality. Hence, as we shall see, Cartmel had a fairly large domestic staff which was the more necessary since the number of brethren here was never very large.

The latter had often special duties to perform. Their head was the prior who possessed a very considerable degree of authority; his deputy being the sub-prior. One of the brethren would, as sacristan, be responsible for the care of the church and its ornaments; the precentor would regulate the church music; the guest-master have charge over the dispensation of hospitality, whilst the infirmerar would look after those of his brethren who were on the sick list. A few manuscripts have survived which give us the full text of the detailed regulations or "observances" by which the life of the medieval regular canons in England was controlled. One of these, full of fascinating detail, has been printed in full, along with an English translation, and to it should refer the reader wishing to have some clear-cut picture of life which prevailed at Cartmel priory during the Middle Ages – this is "The observances in use at the Augustinian priory ... at Barnewell". ed. J. W. Clark (Cambridge 1897).

Architectural History

Although the scrappy evidence which survives does not suffice to enable us to reconstruct a detailed picture of the architectural development of Cartmel, the general outline of its history can be reconstructed and falls into three periods.

(1) c. 1190–c. 1250

The first of these began with the foundation of the priory in or about 1190 and probably continued until about the middle of the following century. The first essential which faced the new canons was to find a suitable site on which to erect their conventual church and the complex series of buildings connected with it.[3] This was not always a very simple matter for them, as it was essential to have an area which offered two major necessities – an abundant water supply (to provide drainage and drinking water, fill the fishponds and work the all essential mill) and a largish piece of flattish and well-drained ground on which to erect the complex series of buildings that were necessary. The only sizable water supply in the whole valley was that supplied by the rather modest beck known as the Ay. In the earlier part of its course down the valley past Broughton it was of very minor dimensions, whilst as it moved towards Cark it got involved in much very low and ill-drained land. But medieval men were practical people and in the end the monastery was built on what was the best site for it which the valley provided, even though experience was ultimately to show that it was not all that could be desired.

The priory church with its attendant cloister buildings were erected on some slightly raised land which had the Ay on its western side and on the east, a small beck which perversely, but inoffensively, decided to flow for a short distance in the opposite direction. The raised land apparently consists principally of a large bed of peat with no solid base, whilst the area near it, even if undesirable for building purposes, had wells supplying excellent water in the fields between the east wall of the churchyard and Causeway End. Although the site chosen might seem an unpromising place in which to erect a massive monastic church, there is no doubt that the medieval builders here were shrewder than some modern ones and that the foundations of their church have caused remarkably little trouble down to our own day.

It is possible that temporary buildings of wood were erected here very soon after the priory had been founded, in which case it may well be that at an early stage the temporary chapel of the brethren was built on the site of what later became known as the Town Choir. The main cloister door, which still remains within the church porch, would be one of the first things to be constructed, and the lower parts of the present chancel would also be an early priority.

However, there can be no doubt that rapid erection of the elaborate cruciform building which contemporary habit regarded as essential for all good monasteries, was well beyond the resources of our district whose inhabitants were neither numerous nor affluent. The indulgence granted by the archbishop of York in 1230 noted above is an unmistakable sign that building operations were then behind schedule, though unhappily we have no means of telling what progress had been made by this time. There is reason to believe that it was not found possible to complete the monastic church at Cartmel on the scale originally planned. It is very likely that only two aisle-less bays of the nave were built and certain that plans to continue the triforium around it were dropped. Such an incomplete church seems strange to modern eyes, but was no rare occurrence in thirteenth-century England.

[3] On the layout of a monastery at this time see J. C. Dickinson, *Monastic Life in Medieval England*.

The eastern side of the cloister building with its refectory, dormitory and chapter-house was probably begun early and finished before the other sides of the cloister (which would be erected in the normal position in the angle between the south transept and the south wall of the nave). On the south side of the cloister, parallel with the nave, would have run the refectory (similar in disposition to that still to be seen at Carlisle cathedral, though on a less lavish scale). On the west side would be the prior's private apartments and some guest accommodation. Probably to the south would be a small infirmary for aged and sick brethren. We know very little of the chronology of the building of this section. But the refectory, infirmary and cloisters mentioned in the visitation of 1281 were almost certainly then complete.

Although the church and cloisters were the focal point of the monastery there were two other major groups of buildings here. One of these satisfied agricultural necessities, notably the barns in which the brethren stored the grain which constituted so very important an element of their food supply throughout the year. Alongside were stables and sheds for the farm stock and implements and other buildings certainly stood around a court called Barngarth, whose name has survived, though very little of its medieval structures can now be clearly identified (see p. 83); a survey of 1508 speaks of some shops in Barngarth. In medieval times the fields north of Causeway End were probably largely used for agriculture as they still are; no little pasture and arable land on the site of the priory is recorded in the survey of 1535.

On the other side of the priory cloister and at some distance west of it, were a more variegated collection of buildings. The most imposing and picturesque of these, and the only one to survive the Reformation virtually intact, is the gatehouse of the priory, evidently constructed about 1330-40 at a time when the ferocious Scottish raids of 1316 and 1322 had sent the Lake Counties into a flurry of fortification. The little road that passes through it northward from the market place had a much altered series of buildings, most of which were originally connected with the heavy responsibilities of the monastery as a land owner and dispenser of hospitality, which will be considered below (see p. 40). All these various complexes were separated from the outside world by a lofty precinct wall which was largely rebuilt and partly re-sited in the fifteenth century. Scattered around the village, built into walls at odd places, are a number of medieval carved stones, almost all of which show types of ornament in vogue in the middle decades of the thirteenth century.

(2) c. 1330-c. 1340

The second building period in the history of Cartmel priory was limited in time and extent, covering (very roughly) the fourth decade of the fourteenth century and concerning only the priory gatehouse, already mentioned, and the Town Choir, or as it used to be called "the Harrington Choir". The latter replaced a small vaulted chapel exactly the same as that still surviving on the north side of the chancel and known as the Piper Choir. But somewhere about 1340 it was rebuilt on a large scale by Lord John Harrington, member of the major local family which at this time owned nearby Wraysholme Tower as well as Gleaston Castle near Ulverston and who died in 1347. The old chapel was now completely destroyed and a longer and wider building put in its place, with singularly attractive windows and exquisite stained glass, a good portion of which happily remains. Probably at the western end of the chapel was placed a chantry chapel which had the effigies of Sir John and his wife Joan (*née* Dacre) at the western end and an altar at the other, whereat a priest would say mass for the good of their souls, of which attractive battered remains have survived (see p. 36). It is worthy of note that the Town Choir was also intended for use as the place of worship of the parishioners, as its predecessor had almost certainly been; it would almost certainly have preserved the dedication to St Michael which had belonged to the church which existed in the valley before the foundation of the priory, though this dedication has been lost for centuries.

(3) *c. 1400-c. 1450*

The third phase of building operations at the priory was very important, constituting the only major reconstruction which it has ever received. It is highly probable that this new work began either in the final years of the fourteenth century, when, as we have seen, it was asserted that the priory buildings were in ruinous condition, or very soon after that date. So far as the conventual church is concerned, the most important change was the replacement of the old nave by a larger one of very plain and cheap construction. But there had evidently also been some little trouble with the foundations of the crossing which, though much less serious than that which caused major trouble at Furness and Fountains at this time, led to the easternmost pier of the crossing being partially rebuilt. Now also, the chancel was given some modest triforium windows. More important and spectacular was the importation of the magnificent east window some 48 feet by 24, to be considered later.

The other major addition was a notable one which gave the priory church its unique external appearance. This was the square belfry tower now constructed diagonally across the original lantern tower, which was now slightly refurbished. This simple and striking design has received both praise and blame from the aesthetes. Almost certainly the main reasons for it were partly the need to spare expense at a time when the church and cloister were in great need of repair (an elaborate tower of the type constructed at this period at Fountains or Furness, would almost certainly have been beyond Cartmel's means), but partly also the solidly practical one of limiting the strain on the piers of the crossing.

The church thus reconstructed had been made very safe for future generations who have never since needed to engage in any major construction of it. The brethren went on to beautify its interior. The most spectacular achievement was the acquisition of stained glass for the mighty east window, inserted about 1420-30 and almost certainly inspired by that at York Minster completed a little earlier. Notable also was the new set of choir stalls (*c.* 1430-40) of which the seats and benches remain largely intact, though the old canopies were replaced in the early seventeenth century. At the same time two sizeable new windows were inserted in each transept. From this time onwards, there was to be no major change in the architecture of the priory church.

The reconstruction and re-adornment of the conventual church in the first half of the fifteenth century was of great delight to the generations who saw it under way and to those thousands who have seen its final form. Much more radical and expensive for those faced with the situation at the time were the changes wrought with regard to the cloister and its domestic buildings. By a decision which is almost, if not quite, unique in the history of English medieval monastic architecture, the brethren of Cartmel now found it necessary to undertake the immensely inconvenient and expensive task of removing the cloister court from its position in the south of the church and rebuilding it *in toto* on the north side of the church. So very heavy a task would never have been undertaken by an unplutocratic monastery as Cartmel priory, without the most urgent necessity. The papal bull of 1390 was almost certainly correct in asserting that the priory buildings were in ruinous condition and the present writer has very little doubt that this was largely due to the fact that the foundations of the cloister buildings had proved defective. As had been noted these were laid on a bed of peat and there is no doubt that there were dangerous springs of water nearby then, as there are now. However this may be, it is certain that, in or about the early decades of the fifteenth century, the priory engaged on the immensely expensive transference of the cloister court and attendant buildings, to the north side of the church as part and parcel of the great overhaul. It is unfortunate that once again we have little precise chronological information of the course of operations. The papal bull probably led to their commencement soon after its reception at Cartmel, whilst the will of Sir William Harrington of 1457 with its financial help to the priory towards building expenses was probably made towards the end of what was certainly a lengthy operation. The fact that the stained glass of the east window can be dated to about 1420-30, gives us a small clue to the rate of progress. One or two interesting indications of the priory's need for thrift at this time can be discerned in certain small alterations, which will be noted later.

The original cloister on the south side of the church having been demolished, the whole area here now became a public cemetery having in its midst the usual preaching cross, of which the lower part still remains. As all, or most of this area had hitherto been used for secular purposes, this would entail the consecration of ground for use as a cemetery, one of the ceremonies reserved to a bishop, but the record of when this was done is not known to have survived. Probably also, there was some reconstruction outside the southwest corner of the church where a small gateway was probably built spanning the road between the present Priory Shop and the churchyard wall. A passage led through this to a small court which had on its western side the prior's apartments (much of whose walls are probably embedded in the large house now called Priory Close), with other buildings nearby including what was perhaps a guest house having stabling below and sleeping accommodation above, reached by a stair and a small door recently revealed. The very short nave had no great western entrance as one might have expected it to have, but only a very small door under the great window which must have been primarily intended for the private use of the prior and his household.

Of the buildings which hemmed in the cloister, and of the cloister arcade, nothing

Plate 3 — Stained Glass in Cartmel Priory Church.

a. An Archbishop (? St. William of York).

b. Rod of Jesse *(detail)*.

c. Arms of Cartmel Priory *(parti per pale or et vert, a lion rampant gules)*.

Plate 4 — Choir Stalls in Cartmel Priory Church.

remains, but it would follow the stock plan with chapter-house and dormitory on the east side; the refectory on the side opposite the church and probably guest accommodation on the west side. North of the church is a field on the east side of the vicarage garden that is called "Farmery field" through having formerly had in it the monastic infirmary. Of this and other structures, traces are very visible in recent air-photographs. To the west, between Farmery field and the beck were probably gardens and orchards with fields further away to the north. At the point where the path along the east side of the churchyard reaches the road leading to Priest Lane was probably a small gateway near which, in Farmery field some skeletons were found some thirty years ago. They probably belonged to the lay cemetery which was on this side of the church until the cloisters were removed (p. 83).

The Dissolution of Cartmel Priory

The suppression of the monasteries of Lancashire under Henry VIII has recently been luminously studied by Dr Christopher Haigh, whose work has made it possible to see for the first time all the main details of this protracted and stormy process. The rights and wrongs of this Dissolution have long been debated, but modern historical research has brought very near an agreed solution hereon. No-one would now maintain that the dominant motive for the Suppression was anything else than a greedy wish to divert monastic wealth into the royal treasury, nor can the antique allegations of the highly corrupt life of monastic inmates now command acceptance. There were certainly needs in certain areas for spiritual amelioration, but the same could be said of non-monastic societies, not least that of the Tudor laity who have so far largely escaped the attentions of the historians' moral microscope. Most of these competent to judge today would accept the dictum of the eminent Protestant historian G. G. Coulton who wrote "The Religious Orders have been among the main forces of European civilisation: at certain times and at certain places they may perhaps have been the greatest of civilising forces".

It has long been realised that the conditions of English monasteries at this time, whether economic, social or spiritual, varied not a little from house to house and to area. It would now appear that in important ways the condition of North Lancashire monasteries in general, was well above average. Of our priory Haigh writes "the general condition of Cartmel was apparently good . . . there was obvious enthusiasm for the religious life and the house was still attracting recruits" and he also notes its useful part in the social life of the county; "functions important enough to raise a rebellion when the house was attacked". In some areas the revolt against the Dissolution had strong economic motives behind it, but in Lancashire he notes that the main root of opposition "must be sought among religious ideas, and particularly opposition to the dissolution of the monasteries".

Early in 1536 the obsequious Parliament of the time passed the Act for the Suppression of the smaller English monasteries. Commissioners to put the Act into effect were quickly appointed, and those concerned with Cartmel arrived there in June. The priory complained that the 1535 valuation of its income was too small, so a new valuation was made which proved their point, its assessment now being raised to £212. 12s. 10½d. a figure which moved them out of the official category of "smaller monasteries". Amongst the items of this survey an interesting one records oblations at a relic of the Holy Cross preserved in the priory. As to other assets of the house, bells, lead and goods were valued at £264. 13s. 9½d. with debts to the house at £59. 12s. 8d. The staff of the monastery included a brewer, baker, cook, scullion, butler, millers, woodmen, fisherman, wright, forester, poulterer and malt maker, two shepherds, two woodsmen and eight farm labourers, the total being thirty-eight. These would, of course, serve the needs not only of the brethren, but of its fairly numerous dependents and guests. The names and ages of the brethren of the house are carefully noted. These were Richard Preston, prior, 41; James Eskeridge, Subprior, 36; William Pennel, 68; Richard Backhouse, 41; John Rudley, 32; Austin Fell, 33; Thomas Briggs, 30; Thomas Parson, 35; Brian Willan, 28; and John Cowper, 25 – the preponderance of youngish men is worthy of note.

Sensing the disaster ahead, the parishioners of Cartmel now sought to preserve at least their own heritage, claiming successfully as their property a set of copes, a chalice and other necessities for the maintenance of their worship, which, of course had no legal connection with that of the monastery. Immensely important for the future was their major claim to retain the priory church as being "also the parish church". This was something of a half-truth, since a part of the priory church had been conventual, not parochial. It would not have been surprising if Cartmel folk had only been allowed to retain the nave – i.e. that part of the church which in no few other religious houses had long been used as their place of worship by the parishioners, as occurred at this time at Bolton priory and Lanercost. But, their request for the whole church was completely successful, it being "ordered by Mr. Chancellor of the Duchy that it (the church) stand still". This unusual decision in such a case was perhaps partly dictated by the desirability of being conciliatory in an area where conservative feeling was very strong, but probably also because the parishioners had also had traditional access to worship in the Town Choir and south transept. The immensely cheering result of it was that Cartmel became one of the very tiny minority of such places where the old monastic church in its entirety was now preserved from the total or semi-ruin which overtook the rest, by being transferred *in toto* to the parishioners.

The commissioners sent up to London the valuables of the monastic community and expelled the brethren from the priory but did not make provision for them to continue their monastic life, elsewhere, as all or possibly all but one of them at Cartmel had expressed the wish to do so (herein displaying a very high spiritual morale which was by no means universal at this time).

Though it is possible that details of the sale of the priory's goods still exist in the Public Records Office, they have not yet been discovered. However there is no doubt that stained glass from the priory went elsewhere almost certainly at this time, probably being taken from the cloister and its attendant buildings and still to be seen in the neighbouring churches of St Martin's Windermere (Bowness) (see pp. 87-8) and St Anthony's Cartmel Fell (see pp. 86-7).

By now in Lincolnshire and much of northern England, local indignation at the suppression of monasteries now going on apace, boiled over into a revolt, or rather a series of local rebellions, known as the Pilgrimage of Grace. This indignation was, apparently, unusually strong in Lancashire North of the Sands. Here the brethren of Cartmel and Conishead (the only two local monasteries as yet affected by the Dissolution) were re-installed in their cloisters, in the early days of October 1536, apart from the prior of Cartmel, who, perhaps feeling that opposition to the government was hopeless, fled south of the Sands. A few Cartmel men including Michael Thornburgh (presumably from Hampsfield Hall) went to York to discuss the situation with insurgent leaders there. Strong local feeling in support of the brethren kept them safely ensconced for some time and in December their right to continue in their monasteries was understood to be conceded by an official, who, however, probably never intended to do more than play for time.

But trouble was soon sparked off at Cartmel where the lands of the legally dissolved priory had been quickly leased to Thomas Holcroft, one of the many individuals who at this time were working busily to feather their own nests with the aid of confiscated monastic property. When he and his helpers arrived here and attempted to remove corn from the priory barns – probably principally the "great barn" then standing in Barngarth – certain canons and husbandmen not only regarded this as an attack on property which rightfully belonged to the priory (whatever arbitrary royal officials might say) but put their conviction into practice by forcibly preventing removal of the corn. At this time the rapacious government of Henry VIII lived in an acute state of anxiety over opposition to its measures, which it strove to allay in the perennial totalitarian manner, by displays of ferocious violence, for which it sought legalistic authority, defining treason in scandalously wide terms quite alien to English legal tradition. Technically those who had here opposed Holcroft could thus be charged with being traitors.

By the opening months of 1537 it was becoming clear that the force behind the Pilgrimage of Grace was disintegrating and martial law was vigorously employed on the disorganised and dis-spirited rebels by a badly frightened government. Opposition to the Dissolution at Cartmel had been particularly resolute and its ringleaders were now sought. Nine canons of Cartmel – virtually the whole convent, except the prior – and sixteen husbandmen were indicted on charges of treason. Three of these canons succeeded in escaping arrest and were early said to be in hiding near Kendal. One of them, James Eskrigge, the subprior, pertinaciously made his way to Scotland where he continued to live out the monastic life in the priory of Holyrood. Of the later history of the other two – John Rudley and Thomas Person – nothing is known. Three of the indicted husbandmen also escaped trial. They were James Stanes, Mile Deconson and John Deconson, who may well have belonged to the family of that name now residing at Wraysholme.

The rest of those indicted were brought to trial at Lancaster early in March accused of treason. Two canons – Thomas Brigge and Brian Willan – were acquitted, as were three of the husbandmen – Richard Gardener, Richard Nuby and John Neylson. In due course Thomas Brigge was given a chaplaincy at Ulverston and Brian Willan became parish priest of Cartmel. Menwhile the ex-prior had been given a substantial pension and a lease of the rectory at Cartmel. All the rest of those accused were found guilty and hung at Lancaster. In days when great sacrifice for high principles is rarish, the names are worthy of being held in remembrance.

They are:

Canons
Augustine Fell   Richard Backhouse
William Panell   John Cowper

Husbandmen
Robert Dawson   John Byglond
Peter Barwyk   John Brokbank
Matthew Bateman   William Crossefeld
James Carter   William Byrkhed
John Blackhead   Gilbert Preston

The Aftermath

After the priory was dissolved in 1536-7, as before, the spiritual care of the parishioners was principally in the hands of a stipendiary chaplain. The last pre-Reformation chaplain was succeeded in office by a former canon of the priory Brian Willan who apparently held office for the best part of half a century, dying in 1589. Cartmel church life in his time must have been very conservative and this is confirmed by the memorial in the south transept put up to Etheldred Thornburgh (called after an Anglo-Saxon abbess) which ends with a prayer for her soul, at times when this was not approved by the Anglican authorities. Unhappily there was no fixed endowment for the priest in charge, as no vicarage had been created in medieval times, the priory having been licensed to appoint to office either a hired secular priest or one of their own brethren. The rectory of Cartmel with its extensive tithes provided a potential source of payment but was largely used for other purposes, passing into the hands of the bishops of Chester, 1557-8 (to whose diocese our area *inter alia* now was transferred), who rented out the rectory to the local squires – the Prestons of Holker. A vicarage with adequate fixed endowment was only very slowly acquired. In 1856 Cartmel was moved to the diocese of Carlisle in which it still remains.

At the time of the Dissolution there were probably only two chapels in Cartmel valley whereat the faithful could attend mass. The earliest of these, naturally enough, was at Flookburgh where the road over the sands to Furness and South Cumberland brought a smallish but steady flow of traffic (see p. 89). The second chapel was at Cartmel Fell and had been established only thirty or forty years before the Dissolution. Other small chapels came slowly. One at Lindale may have originated before the end of the sixteenth century and that of Staveley-in-Cartmel a little later but this is uncertain. At Broughton a humble edifice was founded by 1745 but Allithwaite and Grange had to wait much longer.

At Cartmel itself the dissolution of the monastery was followed by the establishment of a body of Twenty Four, men elected by the various sub-divisions of the great parish who managed the business affairs of the church. The minute book of their meetings from 1597 onwards has most happily survived and gives us an immense amount of invaluable information. It shows amongst other things, that in the early seventeenth century the church was by no means ruinous, as has been too often stated, but that the problem of its upkeep, notably care of its mighty roofs was straining local resources to the utmost. Most of the priory estates had been acquired by the branch of the pious Preston family then at Holker, whose head, George Preston, now came to the rescue. He made an agreement with the Twenty Four whereby a wide-ranging restoration of the church was undertaken. For this the latter levied four compulsory rates of twenty marks each on the faithful between 1618 and 1623, and Mr Preston subscribed a great deal of money – the precise extent of his liberality is unknown, but was certainly immense, going far beyond mere necessities. As a result the roof of the church was extensively repaired within and without, and the chancel and Town Choir were given attractive moulded plaster ceilings of the type much in vogue in local country houses, as we may still see at Levens Hall. Most important of all was the re-furbishing of the fifteenth-century choir stalls. The upper parts of these, almost certainly correctly, were judged to be beyond repair and were now replaced by new ones of very classical design, albeit incorporating no few medieval motifs. These have a sophistication and grace which puts them amongst the finest woodwork of seventeenth-century England [Pl. 4]. Local tradition is almost certainly correct in asserting that these were the work of Flemish carvers who may well have landed at Piel where the elder branch of the Preston family, then resident at Furness abbey, possessed what was almost the only good harbour for many miles around and through which they maintained links with the Continent. In addition to these benefactions George Preston erected on the reconstructed choir screen what his quaint epitaph terms "a pair of organes of great valewe".

Alongside this major effort to improve the church came minor but not unimportant ones. In 1613 much of the south wall of the nave was reconstructed. The porch was reconstructed "in the same place where formerlye it was" in 1626, and ten years later the church was provided "a fitt and decent raile about the communion table". Most unhappily in 1643 Cromwellian soldiers spent a night at Cartmel, smashing up the new organ in their inhibited way, stabling their horses in the nave of the church and probably destroying much stained glass and overthrowing local crosses. In 1660 came the re-establishment of Anglicanism. The font was now re-erected in its ancient place, a copy of the last edition of the Book of Common Prayer ordered and – in 1661 – the bells re-cast. In 1677 came the last architectural change of note when, in accordance with a bequest by Mr William Robinson of Newby Bridge, there was constructed "a new vestry and questhouse over the same . . . the present vestry being a small and low building unproportionable to the rest of the said church". In the same year the vicar of Cartmel John Armstrong had printed at Cambridge for his parishioners "Secret and family prayers... for the use of... the inhabitants of Cartmel" [Pl. 14a]. A small collection of books had already been acquired and are mentioned as being chained in the church in the early seventeenth century but in 1697 the will of Mr Thomas Preston led to its acquisition of his very extensive library. This comprised some 300 volumes mostly printed between 1525 and 1660 and of a theological nature; the only literary item of any note was a first edition of part of Spenser's *Faerie Queen* (1596, STC 28082), which in 1929 was stolen from the vestry but returned to Cartmel after having been unavailingly offered for sale in New York.

In these times few folk attracted more controversy than George Fox, the founder of the Quakers, who was well known in the area, through him having made his headquarters at Swarthmoor Hall near Ulverston, the home of his wife Margaret Fell. In 1653 his journal records "Priest Bennett of Cartmel sent a challenge to dispute with me. Hereupon I came to his steeple house on a First day and found him preaching. When he had done I spoke to him and his people, but the priest would not stand his trial and went his way. After he had gone I had much discourse with the people". In 1677 the Quakers of the area erected a meeting house charmingly set on the heights above Newton which acquired its own cemetery but is now disused.

Within the old priory church during the seventeenth century the area under and near the crossing was elaborately adapted for the Anglican worship of the day in which a dominant feature was the "three decker pulpit", from which the priest took prayers, read the lessons and preached the sermon; this was unhappily scrapped by Cartmel Victorians, but a similar one at Cartmel Fell Church is still with us. Now also were to be seen several very bulky private pews acquired by leading families of the parish, notable being that of the Dicconsons of Wraysholme Tower who had the brilliant idea of putting it on large castors (two of which remain) thus allowing it to be shifted out of draughts or into sunlight.

In the eighteenth century there was little to note in the history of the church, though in 1759, as we shall see, John Wesley passed through Flookburgh on his way into Cumberland and did not find things to his liking (see pp. 46-7). Cheap pews for the lower orders were added now, some being perched on high, but the financial strain which maintenance of the huge church put on the small and scattered population of the valley became evident again, even if the writer who in 1818 described the place as "something between a cathedral and a ruin" was certainly guilty of exaggeration.

Happily under the Rev. Thomas Remington, senior fellow of Trinity College, Cambridge who was vicar of Cartmel from 1835 to 1854, a vigorous campaign for its restoration got under way which finished only in 1870; this put the church in first class condition albeit by measures which, as was so often the case at this time, were a good deal more radical than modern opinion would approve. The ancient three-decker and family pews were scrapped as were the singularly picturesque plaster ceilings put in by the good Mr Preston. Very necessarily however the floor of the church was flattened out, and the great roofs restored. It is a remarkable fact that even now the foundations of the church were still as firm as they had been when laid by the builders seven centuries before, and indeed right down to the present have needed no major attention. The Rev. Thomas Remington gave the faithful their first heating apparatus. The windows in the transepts acquired late Victorian stained glass of admirable quality mostly by Shrigley and Hunt of Lancaster. The sanctuary was given rather horrific Victorian tiling and a mighty gilt reredos of apostles donated by Lady Louisa Egerton which failed to retain the admiration of posterity. In recent times no major problems of maintenance have arisen, apart from the need to clean and repair the medieval stained glass in the great east window and the Town Choir, which was recently most successfully effected by Mr Dennis King. For long the organ was perched picturesquely over the entrance to the quire screen but the Victorians unhappily encumbered the exquisite Town Choir with a new one, a mistake that has recently been repeated, albeit on a somewhat smaller scale.

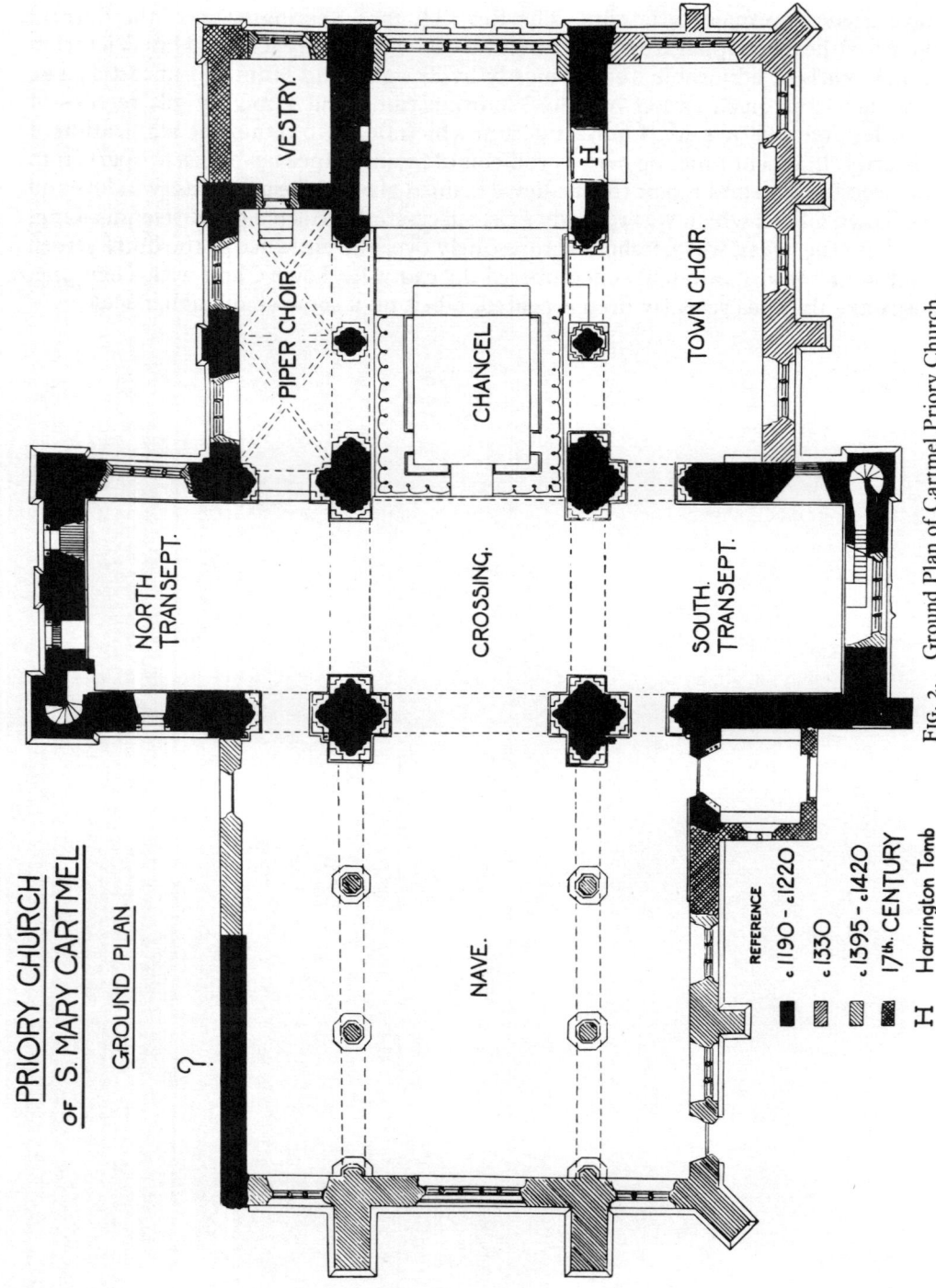

Fig. 2. Ground Plan of Cartmel Priory Church.

CHAPTER THREE

THE PRIORY CHURCH TODAY

THE main gateway to the churchyard and priory church lies southwest of the latter and is modern. Just outside it until a century or so ago were the mounting-block, which was no little employed by the faithful of the valley until motor cars replaced horses for transport, and the stocks in which were pinned locals guilty of minor misbehaviour (Pl. 1) and which fell into disuse in Victorian times, their timbers being finally given to his lady-love by the local policeman, if tradition is correct. Much of the northern half of the present churchyard was originally covered by the monastic cloister and its attendant buildings, and would have been consecrated for its present use when the latter were moved to the north side of the church in the early part of the fifteenth century. To this period belongs also the weathered stump of the churchyard cross still therein to be seen some fifty yards south of the porch. William Taylor, a local lad and a former fellow of Emmanuel College Cambridge, became headmaster of the admirable school at Hawkshead when the poet William Wordsworth was a pupil there and finally at Cartmel. His gravestone stands between the old sundial (whose dial of 1727 has been purloined) and the western wall of the churchyard.

In the southern face of the south transept of the church at first floor level is a blocked door which originally gave access to the church from the monastic dormitory which adjoined it here. In the west wall adjoining it are relics of the old cloisters, including parts of its stone bench and two of the corbels which supported its lean-to roof. The shallow oblong recess here probably originally contained a carved panel of some sacred subject which in the fifteenth century replaced a semi-circular headed recess wherein were kept books in use in the cloister.

Most of the south wall of the nave of the church, like the rest of the nave, belongs to the early part of the fifteenth century, but part of its eastern end has been rebuilt, probably in the seventeenth century. The little doorway at the west end of this wall was for the use of the parishioners, and happily retains its traceried and heavily studded oak door. In this are several large holes which local tradition avers to be bullet holes fired in by local folk at Cromwellian soldiers who had stabled their horses in the nave. It is quite certain that Parliamentarian soldiery stopped briefly at Cartmel in Oct. 1643 after having won a skirmish against Royalist forces at Lindal-in-Furness and it is most interesting to note that when this "Cromwell Door" (as it is traditionally termed) was restored in very recent years fragments of lead were found in the above-mentioned holes. In the gable at the west end of the church is a bell cot which has lost its bell, and which probably originally was for the use of the parishioners. The present porch was built in 1626 on the site of one which may well have been a couple of centuries older; it encloses a magnificent doorway which originally gave access to the church from the first cloister. Made in the last years of the twelfth century it has a typical mixture of Romanesque and early Gothic features. If local tradition is correct the hollow in one of its pillars was worn away by generations of local "dog-whippers" (officials now extinct, who were given a small sum to ensure that dogs did not join the faithful in divine worship, and who are known to have existed at Cartmel).

The Nave (c. 1430)

The main door gives access to the present nave of the church which retains next to no signs of the original one which was probably quite short and not intended to be permanent. This one was clearly built in times of stringency, being shortish and plain with walls whose simple rubble walling contrasts markedly with the elegant ashlar of the older parts of the church. The roof and the glass in the windows are all Victorian, as is the present unattractive font. This replaces an early thirteenth century one which, as old prints show us clearly was set here on a fine set of steps which were unhappily destroyed in the restoration of the last century when also the bowl of the font itself was dis-figured by being re-cut; after being lent to Flookburgh church it was returned to Cartmel, being at present located in the Town Choir. The curious cover was made in 1640; its early blue and gilt colouring has very recently been restored. In the floor near the new font is the gravestone of one Nicholas Barrow with an inscription that includes the non-committal statement "what sort of a man he was, the Last Day will discover".

In the nave are two notable pieces of sculpture. Near the Cromwell door is "They fled by night" by Josephina da Vasconcellas, recently presented by Sydney Walton. It depicts the Blessed Virgin, with St Joseph and the Child Jesus during their flight into Egypt. In the north west corner of the nave is the memorial to Lord Frederick Cavendish who was murdered on 6 May 1882 in Dublin whither he had gone from Holker a few days before. The fine effigy of him is in Carrara marble the work of Thomas Woolner and rests on a chest of Derbyshire and Cornish marble. Nearby on the north wall are to be seen several funeral hatchments of the Lowther and Cavendish families which in turn inherited the ex-priory lands originally acquired by the Preston family; the Cavendish arms feature three stags' heads and have the motto *Cavendo Tutus*. Near them is the smallish but interesting painted canvas memorial to early members of the Preston family of Holker, including that great benefactor to Cartmel George Preston, who, it records, "out of his zeale to God, at his great charges, repaired this church, being in greate decay, with a newe roofe of tymber and beautified it within very decently with fretted plaister worke, adorned the chancel with curiously carved wood worke and placed therein a pair of organs of greate valewe".

In the west wall of the nave is a small door that communicated with the prior's lodging which by an unusual arrangement stood almost due west of the church. In the north-east corner of the nave by one of the piers of the crossing a small brass memorial to Mr Rowland Briggs of Swallowmire (in Cartmel Fell) record his bequests of £5 "to be laid out in bread and distributed to the most indigent housekeepers of this parish every Sunday for ever" (a charity still maintained) and an annual payment of 5s. "to the sexton and his successors ... to be pay'd every Christmas day provided they keep his grave unbroken up". Close to this is a Victorian alms box with its lid carved to illustrate the parable of the Good Samaritan.

Eastwards from here is the *NORTH TRANSEPT* (c. 1220) which is part of the original building. Its west wall retains the sole original lancet window still in the church. Opposite it is a curious window confected out of the stones of twin lancets, doubtless as an economy measure in the fifteenth century, at which time the large window in its northern wall (which has Victorian glass), was inserted. The removal of the cloisters to the north side led to the lower pair of lancets below this window being blocked up and the old dormitory door from the opposite transept being inserted for re-use in one of them. Probably because of financial stringency, the triforium was not extended to the transepts but an internal wall passage runs right round them and was intended to be extended into the nave, though this was never done. The small doors with corbels on either side high up in the west wall of both transepts were probably originally built to serve in building operations. In the north transept hangs the banner of Sir Evan MacGregor, Knight Grand Cross of the Order of the Bath, who lived at Aynsome. In the floor beneath the pews here may still exist a small stone slab inscribed *Hic Deum Adora* ("Here adore God") mentioned by Victorian writers.

East of the transept and entered through a picturesque arch is the North Choir aisle, traditionally called the *PIPER CHOIR* (c. 1220) for reasons unknown. Most of this with its austere ribbed vaulting belongs to the Transitional style of architecture in vogue when Cartmel Priory was first begun, but the two windows are of fifteenth century date and contain a little of their original glass that includes small representations of the Fathers of the Church. On the wall near them is a marble tablet commemorating members of the Myers family, including one William who is there recorded as having died on the non-existent date of 30 February 1762, according to a text which has been repainted as a joke by some local, who probably also feloniously erased in the parish register the date of William's death, because the latter, it is clear therefrom, occurred well before the end of the month. Here are three medieval tomb slabs, and near them the two enormous castors made for the family pew of the Dicconsons of Wraysholme Tower. The pier at the east end of the chapel has a small piscina and a niche for a statue, but no sign of the altar to which they pertained, remains. Nearby is the memorial of the donor of the vestry, who also left £20 to be invested and the interest paid to "the carter or guide of the sands called Kent sands".

The Vestry (1677)

Probably about the middle of the fifteenth century a small sacristy was added in the angle between the chancel wall and the east end of the Piper choir which had a small south door which gave access to the sanctuary. After the dissolution of the priory, when as we have seen control of local affairs had passed into the hands of the Twenty Four, this was much enlarged for their meetings. For long the upper floor of the vestry housed the church library but recently this has been deposited on loan in the library of Lancaster University.

At present in the vestry are kept some objects of antiquarian interest, of which the most unusual is a large umbrella of painted canvas and oak formerly held over the head of vicars conducting burial services in the rain. Here is an old chair made of wood from the choir stalls to be used also as a parish chest; its hinged lid has the three locks which Anglican law demanded (one for the incumbent and one each for the churchwardens so that all three had to be present before the repository could be opened). Objects in a show-case here include various small fragments of medieval manuscripts, formerly in the bindings of books in the library, some very minor objects found in the Harrington Tomb when it was opened over a century ago, and an ancient key.

To the south of the vestry and Piper Choir lies the *CHANCEL*, where the brethren held their services and which was and is certainly the most magnificent part of the church. Most of it, including the noble arches on either side of it and the little triforium arcade belongs to the original monastic church of *c*. 1190-*c*. 1220 but there were various alterations made here during fifteenth century restoration. Of these the most spectacular was the insertion of the magnificent east window (said to measure 48 ft. by 24 ft.) which replaced the double rows of three lancets which were originally here. This window was quite certainly inspired by the great east window of York Minister and its tracery and glass came from Yorkshire though the great mullions are of local mill-stone grit. The glass which remains is unhappily only a small portion of the original whole; it is of magnificent quality and probably belongs to the period 1420-30. In 1970 it was magnificently restored by Mr Dennis King of Norwich.

In the main lights of the window are still to be found three major panels. In the centre is a representation of Our Lady and the child Jesus, unhappily somewhat damaged, beneath which is a small representation of St Peter enthroned, also not in pristine condition. On the spectator's right is a fine almost perfect picture of St John the Baptist, carrying his emblem the Lamb of God which "taketh away the sins of the world". On the other side of Our Lady is a very benevolent archbishop in red chasuble (Pl. 3a) who may well be Archbishop William of York who died in 1154 and was later canonised. (This figure was originally on the other side of the group but in the recent restoration was moved to its present position.) For details of the glass in the upper part of the window see p. 38.

Originally the triforium arcades in the north and south walls of the chancel were continued to join each other across the east wall, between the two rows of lancets that were originally there. It is not clear what the original clerestory was like, but the present windows there belong to the fifteenth century. The roof timbers are largely modern, like those in the rest of the church. The east end of the chancel, as we have noted, suffered that rigorous restoration to which the Victorians were addicted. There is still visible a very small medieval tombstone on the north side of the sanctuary. Near it is a low arched recess in the north wall which shelters the tombstone of Prior William of Walton of about 1300, which is inscribed HIC JACET FRATER WILLELMUS DE WALTONA PRIOR DE KERTMEL. The modern aumbry in which the Blessed Sacrament is reserved is in the south wall of the sanctuary, its vanished medieval predecessor having been in the opposite corner.

In the southern wall of the sanctuary are to be seen the battered remains of the original piscina and of a fine sedilia of late thirteenth century date. Adjoining the latter are the mutilated but magnificent remains of the "Harrington Tomb", to be described below. The high altar and its attendant candlesticks were acquired some forty years ago. Nearby are two very elaborately carved chairs of seventeenth century date given by the Marquis of Hartington and Lady Louisa Egerton.

At the western end of the chancel are the choir stalls arranged as usual in two L-shaped blocks with the main entrance to the area between them. Adjoining the south side of the latter was the prior's seat; the corresponding one on the north side was allotted to the sub-prior, with the rest of the brethren being seated on either side in order of seniority from west to east. The woodwork here is of two very different dates. The bench-ends, desks and seats are all of the mid-fifteenth century date, but the elaborate pierced screens behind them along with classical columns in front and the canopies overhead were the gift of Mr George Preston, about 1620.

The seventeenth century work is of the highest quality both in design and execution and ranks amongst the finest examples of the period in England. The local tradition that it was done by Flemish craftsmen may well be correct. Although the main design of these screens is strictly classical, with graceful Corinthian columns and pediment, no little of the decoration is in the medieval tradition, notably the various emblems of the Passion of Christ which proliferate. Besides the Cross itself they include the nails and spear thrust into Christ's body, the dice with which the soldiers played, the scourge, the lantern used at the time of the betrayal, the ladder used at the Crucifixion and no few others. Very notable are the hinged and pierced panels of the screens, which are carved in a remarkable variety of designs largely of medieval origin. The symbols of the four evangelists are prominent over the entrance, near which lurk unobtrusively the arms of the Preston family as well as large gold letter quotations from the Psalms. It is interesting to note that some of the timber is re-used, presumably coming from parts of the medieval roof which were still sound.

The Misericords

Of the medieval woodwork one or two of the poppy-head finials which crown the bench-ends of the stalls are badly weather worn, as are, to a much lesser degree, the tops of some of the desks between them. Beneath are the hinged carved seats with their carved brackets beneath (known as "misericords") all in excellent condition. When the seats were turned into an upright position they afforded some little physical support to their users during those considerable parts of the complex services which were expected to be said or sung mostly while standing. As was very usual in the late medieval times, these misericords were carved with a series of designs which were very varied and mostly elaborate, drawn partly from nature (real or imagined) but also from the luxuriant folklore of the time.

The date of the misericords cannot be established with any great precision but stylistic evidence makes it clear that they belong to about the middle of the fifteenth century, possibly to about 1430-40, which makes them just a little less antique than the glass in the great East window. Comparison with their opposite numbers in Carlisle Cathedral and those from Whalley Abbey preserved in Whalley parish church is interesting.

Of the original twenty-six misericords at Cartmel all but one have survived and are, without exception, in excellent condition. Their subjects are as follows, reading from west to east:

South Side

(1) (The prior's seat) – an arabesque design flanked on either side by a letter W, denoting the William who was prior when the seats were inserted.
(2) A crowned head with three noses and three mouths, an arrangement believed in medieval times to characterise the faces of a (mythical) race of giants who lived in India and were called *macrobii*. (Pl. 2a.)
(3) A pelican feeding her young with flesh and blood from her own breast, a symbol of Christ Who gives His Body and Blood to the faithful (Pl. 2c).
(4) A half length figure of an angel holding a shield.
(5) An ape holding a flask – a contemporary mode of satire on doctors, who were held to be as unreliable as monkeys.
(6) A double-tailed mermaid with a comb in one hand and a mirror in the other, from whom, on one side, a fish has turned tail (the mermaid symbolises the lusts of the flesh, the fish the Christian soul which flees from them).
(7) A representation of a crowned figure seated in a large basket to which two large birds are attached. This is a scene from the medieval legend of "Alexander's Flight", according to which the emperor Alexander the Great seeking the end of the world (which was believed to be flat and circular and surrounded by a river) arrived at what he believed to be his goal, and decided to confirm this view by becoming airborne. Two large birds were lashed to a basket into which he mounted, holding a spear bearing a piece of meat which he used as a bait, first to urge the birds upwards till he had seen with his own eyes the world's end, and then to take him back to earth, which they did, albeit depositing him at a place very far from his base. Nearby is carved a capital letter T and on the partition that divides it from the next seat is a curious (?) snare, shaped like a T with a little animal trapped therein.
(8) A dragon passant with flapping wings.
(9) A magnificent peacock with spread tail; on the right is a bat hanging head downwards.
(10) A flying eagle with a bundle of grapes in its beak.

(11) Two large birds eating from a sack (?) of corn.
(12) A grinning mask with leaves.
(13) An elaborate pattern of leaves.

North Side
(1) An oak-tree in the trunk of which a unicorn has embedded its horn, persuading it to do this being held to be one of the few ways that it could be captured.
(2) Leaf design.
(3) A grinning lion mask with foliage coming from its mouth.
(4) (*The seat is lost*)
(5) A griffin passant.
(6) Head of a man with curly hair and beard and whiskers, wearing an ornamental hat.
(7) A large double rose with leaves on either side: on the left is the head of an ox.
(8) A deer chased by three dogs in a wood. (On the left is a crowned monogram of WW with a small heart and flower attached to its terminals, on the right an attractive hedgehog.) (Pl. 2b.)
(9) Three intertwined acanthus leaves.
(10) An elephant and castle leaning against a tree (it was believed that the elephant had no joints in its legs, and slept by leaning against a tree, so could be captured by sawing through part of the trunk against which it was accustomed to seek repose. It hereby resembled Adam who also "fell through a tree".
(11) An elaborate bunch of pendant leaves.
(12) A winged and clawed demon.
(13) A spray of two large leaves.

The medieval organ may have been originally located in the Piper Choir but later, at least, at Cartmel the organ was set across the centre of the choir screen. Here sat the "pair of organes of great valewe" given by Mr Preston, and the later instrument set up in 1817, but, as we have seen, for some time now the noble Town Choir has been cluttered up with a massive ungainly later organ. The high altar of the Chancel, being the major altar of the priory, was dedicated to its patron St Mary, so that we find the chancel anciently called "the Lady Choir".

The Town Choir (c. 1340)

The chapel on the south side of the chancel stands on the site of the early parish altar dedicated to St Michael, and came to be entitled "the Town Choir" since it was originally the place where the local parishioners worshipped. In the *Church Book* we find it also termed "the Harrington quire". As we have seen, it was totally rebuilt by Lord John Harrington (d. 1347) who also added to it the great chantry tomb made for himself and his wife.

It is almost certain that this tomb was originally placed at the west end of the Town Choir with a small altar east of it and an elaborate screen surrounding the whole. At the Reformation the very conservative religious atmosphere in the parish, where, it will be remembered, one of the Cartmel canons continued to work for many years after the dissolution of the priory, probably led to efforts to save this elaborate memorial of the Harringtons.

Though the altar and much of the screen were destroyed (probably by the Roundheads) the effigies of the founder and his wife and the stone chest which contained their mortal remains, as well as a substantial amount of admittedly disjointed arcading survive, as does part of a wooden ceiling of the chantry. They have long formed a rather untidy conglomeration thrust into the wall which separated the east end of the Choir from the sanctuary at the east end of the chancel. On the top of the open stone screen are some loose pieces of medieval sculpture of no great interest and later in date than the Harrington Tomb.

On either side of the effigies are elegant ogee arches somewhat reminiscent of those in the famous Percy tomb in Beverley Minster. The former have in their heads the representations of a soul being drawn up to heaven in a sheet by two angels; above runs a cornice ornamented with foliage. The shafts which support the arches are elaborately carved. The outer ones have at the top a tier of scenes from the life of Christ – on the south side the scourging of Christ and Christ crucified, on the north St Mary Magdalene drying Christ's feet with her hair and Christ blindfolded amongst Pilate's soldiers. Near these are stone shields, scrubbed much too clean by the Victorians, some of which are known to have originally been painted with the coats of arms of Lord John Harrington and his wife Joan (*née* Dacre). Attached to the shafts which support the arch are carved figures. The upper row of these has, on the south side, two of St Michael (blowing the last trumpet) with a blank in between, on the north two censing angels with an unidentified figure between. The lower row – much the more interesting – has on the south side St Peter with the key of Heaven, Our Lady and the Holy Child, St Catherine with her wheel and a niche which is now blank; on the north are St John the Baptist with a plaque of the Lamb of God and (?) St Philip between another empty niche and an unidentified figure. At the corners of the base of the tomb are large emblems of the four Evangelists.

The figures of Lord John and Lady Joan are both about life-size and are shown with uplifted hands which hold a heart, thus literally performing the injunction in the Mass "Lift up your hearts". As was very common with such effigies the feet of the lady rests on a dog, those of her lord and master on a lion. Above them are remains of the original wooden ceiling of the tomb which include two very fine cartoons depicting the symbols of the evangelists St Matthew and St Luke, and slight remains of a coloured representation of Christ in Glory. Around the two effigies are lines of curious little statuettes of Austin canons presumably singing for the souls of the deceased, as are the fascinating little choir of canons sculpted around the base of the stone chest on which the effigies repose, wherein may be seen the precentor beating time with his left hand. The panelling of the chest is very attractive and has on the south side cockle shells, almost certainly because these featured in the arms of the Dacre family.

We do not know the date of the insertion of the remains of the Harrington tomb in its present position. This may have been in the reign of Edward VI when Puritan

Plate 5 — The Land of Cartmel from the map by William Yates 1786.

Plate 6a — Lancaster Sands, from an etching after David Cox.

Plate 6b — The Ulverston to Lancaster Coach (*c.* 1840).

feeling came to run strongly in England or, more likely, in 1643 when Cromwellians were here. Doubtless it was hoped that the move to this position would prevent the total destruction of such remains of it as were then extant, as it certainly did. Just over a century ago the tomb chest was opened but found to contain a very small collection of minute and very miscellaneous remains, of which the only ones now known to survive are preserved in the vestry of the church and are very fragmentary indeed. The tomb was originally painted but little sign of this now remains.

The removal of the remains of the Harrington chantry to its present position necessitated removing from the place in the wall wherein they were to be inserted, an interesting effigy of an Austin canon which already occupied a recess therein. This was moved to the floor below and there remains, little damaged; we do not know whom it commemorates. It shows a canon in choir habit with a long cloak having a very full hood attached and beneath it a rochet (a long white garment). He holds a chalice which, like the pair of angels which support his head and the very lively dragon on which his feet rest are somewhat damaged. Such effigies are very rare indeed though Hexham has one. Its date is uncertain but is almost certainly later than that of the enlargement of the Town Choir.

Probably from the early seventeenth century this chapel for long became in effect the burial place of the Preston and Lowther families which owned Holker Hall; an altar was re-established here early in the present century. Two of the family memorials unhappily partially block the east window of the chapel, a large one of the Prestons and a smallish, elegant one to Sir William Lowther. The east window contains much of its original glass (c. 1340), its main subject being the so-called "Rod of Jesse". It is a pictorial family tree of what was believed to be the earthly genealogy of Christ, some figures here being linked in pairs and their names obligingly provided (Pl. 3b) In the centre of the upper part of the window is preserved an attractive panel showing an angel that was originally linked with the adjoining (lost) one of Our Lady to portray the Annunciation.

In front of the altar are two stout "housel benches", precursors of the modern communion rail. Towards the east end of the south wall is a small sedilia having two seats instead of the usual three; towards the west end of the chapel is the re-cut thirteenth century font and its seventeenth century cover, and the organ. Near the latter almost certainly there originally stood the Harrington chantry. In the central one of the southern windows of the chapel is a little medieval glass, including the arms of the priory (a red lion on a gold and green ground) (Pl. 3c) and those of the Harringtons (a silver "fret" on a black ground). Originally this choir exactly matched the Piper Choir but when it was rebuilt by Lord John Harrington the stone vaulted roof was replaced by a flat timber ceiling (renewed in the Victorian restoration) resting on corbels including one which depicts Samson wrestling with the lion.

West of the Town Choir is the *South Transept*, which most dates to c. 1190-c. 1220, though the two windows in its south wall were inserted after the removal of the cloister buildings to the north side of the church; their excellent Victorian glass was made by Shrigley and Hunt, of Lancaster. Below them is the entrance to a

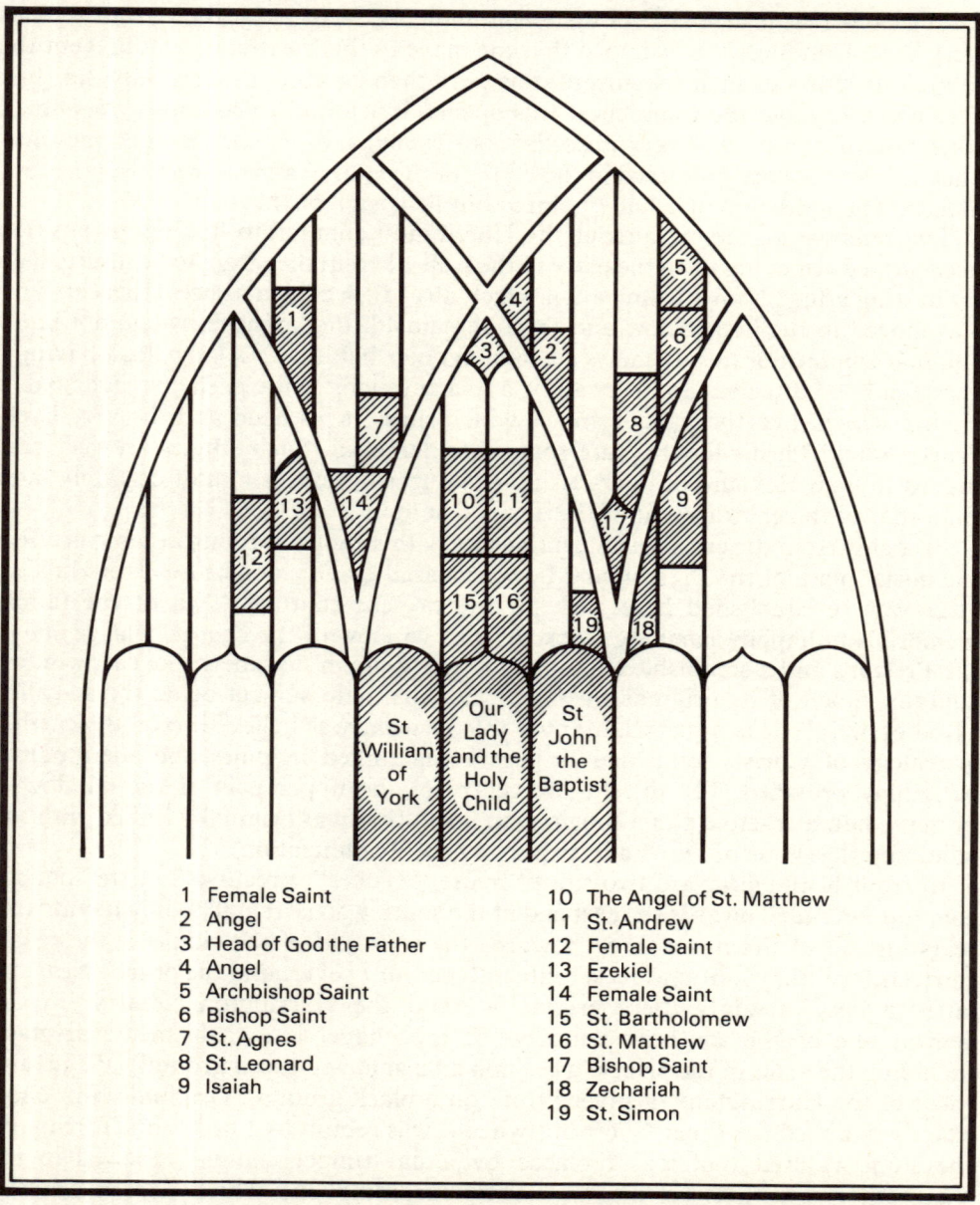

FIG. 3. East Window of Cartmel Priory Church.

stair which leads to the roof and belfry. At the west end of the same wall at first floor level is a blocked opening which originally contained the dormitory door now in the north transept, and from which a flight of stairs originally gave access to the church. Set in the wall near it is a small memorial tablet of Elizabethan date, commemorating a member of one of the Catholic-minded families of the area.

> Here before lyeth interred
> Ethelred Thornburgh corps in dust
> In lyfe at death styll fyrmely fixed
> On God to rest her steadfast trust
> Hir father Justice Carus was
> Hir mother Katherine his wiffe
> Hir husband William Thornburgh was
> Whylst here she ledd this mortall lyfe
> The third of Matche and year of grace
> One thousands fyve hundred nyntie six
> Hir sowle departed this earthly place
> Of aage nighe fortie yeares and six
> To whose sweet sowle heavenlye dwellinge
> Our Savious grant everlastinge.

To the north of the transept are the four great arches of *The Crossing*, which are largely of the 1190-1290 period though the head of the southern one was rebuilt in the fifteenth century. The present wooden ceiling replaced an older one in 1854 and bears the coats of arms of: Cartmel priory (S.W. corner), the Province of York (N.W. corner), Preston of Holker (N.E. corner), and the see of Chester (S.E. corner). In the centre is a handsome brass chandelier given in 1734 by Mrs Margaret Marshall of Aynsome. Immediately above is the picturesque ringing chamber which contains a curious notice giving instructions for the ringers; above is the striking diagonal belfry. It has four ancient bells, two of 1661, one of 1726 and one of 1729, and are those whose singular sweetness inspired Gordon Bottomley's well known poem "Cartmel Bells"; to them two others were added in 1932.

In monastic times the church was surrounded by an elaborate set of *Conventual Buildings* almost all of which have wholly or partially disappeared. Of the monastic cloister and the buildings which adjoined it no significant trace remains, though the buildings near the west end of the nave and running parallel to it, notably the large one (named Priory Close), and the one adjoining it on the north contain no little medieval walling (mostly remains of the prior's house). To the east end of the church, beyond the low-lying land which adjoins it here is Barngarth, where were originally a miscellany of agricultural buildings. The Great Barn of the monastery with shippons beneath vanished long ago and has very recently been partially replaced by a bungalow. The houses on the opposite side of the road to it contain no little ancient walling; one or both of them were probably used to house the secular clergy who mostly attended to the spiritual needs of the parishioners; this accounts for the road north of them being termed "Priests' Lane" and the well in front of them "Priests' Well". The large house to the north of them is probably an into shops. A little gatehouse across the road near here has left no trace. To the west, beyond the small row of cottages near to the north side of the entrance to the churchyard, is a field known as "Farmery field" owing to the monastic infirmary having been built here; remains of it long survived. As we have seen traces of what seems to have been a small cemetery have been found near here, and an air photograph has revealed signs of various minor buildings and a substantial ditch in this area.

The sole major domestic building of the priory to survive the storms of the Reformation virtually intact is the very picturesque *Gatehouse* which dominates the little square a few hundred yards west of the church. This was built about 1330-40 probably as a result of the great scare created in these parts by the Scottish raids of 1316 and 1322, and is rather crudely constructed. The entrance is by a passage of two bays, one a pointed barrel vault, the other groined. On the left of the passage an ogee-headed door leads to what was originally a porter's lodge, and opposite is the entrance to a broad circular stair which gives access to the room which monopolised the first floor and whose principal use was as the court-room of the manor of Cartmel. It has a pair of quite handsome windows of two lights each with ogee heads, transoms and stone benches in its north and south walls, and a substantial fireplace in the western one near which is a small niche probably to hold a crucifix and a wall cupboard, perhaps to house records. A staircase in the north wall led down to the priory precinct and would be used *inter alia* by monastic officials. In 1624, as we have seen, the Twenty Four purchased this gatehouse from Mr Preston to house the school hitherto held in the church. To this time probably belong the large windows in the two gables and probably also the substitution of a slate roof which involved the removal of the battlements and the turret at its south-east angle. It may be also that a loft was now added at the eastern end of the main chamber, though this was not a permanent arrangement. In 1790 it passed into private hands and came to be used for various purposes including a storehouse. Happily after no little neglect in 1923 it was purchased and extensively re-furbished by the late R. O'Neill Pearson who presented it to the National Trust.

Like other ancient crosses in the area the market cross in the land in front of the gate-house, has lost its original head, and the statue in the niche over the entrance has not survived. The steps of the cross are there, as are the fish stones on which, until comparatively recent times, a fine assemblage of the finny tribe were available for purchase. The picturesque little street running north from the gate-house, much beloved by artists and photographers is hemmed by buildings which contain a good deal of monastic walling, though the doors, windows and roofs are all of later date. The Cavendish Arms almost certainly stands on part of the site of a guest-house and the house opposite contained until some forty years ago an enormous old oven which was probably the medieval bakery. The nearby smithy is almost certainly on a medieval site and supplied horse-shoes and, in later times, iron-bound cartwheels for many locals; the bridge round the corner is modern, replacing a small medieval bridge which led originally into the private part of the monastic precinct which contained various fields and orchards.

CHAPTER FOUR

TRAVEL

AS we have seen, the land of Cartmel shared with the neighbouring land of Furness the curious position of having been part of the county of Lancashire from the establishment of the latter eight centuries ago to its dismemberment in 1965, despite the fact that both of them were separated from the major part of the county by the waters of Morecambe Bay. Yet, odd as it may seem to modern eyes, right down to the advent of the railway age the main thoroughfare from Lancaster to Furness and Cartmel was not round the coast but boldly across Morecambe Bay.

Travellers going northward by this route mostly started from Lancaster, the initial stage being a journey over land of some $3\frac{1}{2}$ miles to the coast at Hest Bank, near Bolton-le-Sands. Most folk made the crossing on foot, though the fortunate few might go on horseback or by cart or, later, by coach. The crossing could only be safely undertaken at periods strictly dictated by the constantly changing times of high and low water. The following excerpt from one of the monthly Tide Tables given in the *Lonsdale Magazine* for 1822 displays clearly the complications that this caused the traveller.

Tide Table

"The tides will be found to vary considerably from the proceeding table under the influence of powerful winds; if a strong wind blow with the tide there will be a higher tide, earlier high water and later crossing; but if, on the contrary the wind blow *against the tide*, there will be a lower tide, a later high water, and earlier crossing.

	HIGH WATER Lancaster, Ulverston Grange, Ravenglass		Time of beginning to cross Lancaster and Ulverston Sands			HIGH WATER Lancaster, Ulverston Grange, Ravenglass		Time of beginning to cross Lancaster and Ulverston Sands	
1	0.33	0.50	4.58	5.18	11	8.36	9.12	0.0	0.35
2	1.8	1.18	5.30	5.40	12	9.46	10.12	1.12	1.45
3	1.38	1.50	6.3	6.10	13	10.38	11.3	2.12	2.40
4	2.8	2.18	6.33	6.47	14	11.31	12.51	3.5	3.31
5	2.40	3.15	7.4	7.15	15	0.0	0.15	3.52	4.16
6	3.12	3.31	7.11	7.40	16	0.25	0.58	4.35	4.58
7	3.55	4.16	7.55	8.16	17	1.16	1.40	5.15	5.40
8	4.40	5.11	8.40	9.10	18	2.0	2.22	6.0	6.24
9	5.52	6.29	9.50	10.9	19	2.40	3.2	6.40	7.5
10	7.15	7.57	11.17	11.58	20	3.23	3.45	7.22	7.45"

The distance from Hest Lane to Kent's Bank, which became the main northern terminus of the over-Sands route is some seven miles as the crow flies, but the traveller often had further to go, as the guide might select a longer course in order to secure the best crossing point of the dangerous channel of the river Kent – a guidebook of 1828 gives this route a length of 11 miles. The time taken to effect the journey was thus variable but was often in the region of two and a half hours. As may have been noted, the *Lonsdale Magazine* time-table set the crossing to begin some four and a quarter hours after High Water, but is probably playing for safety, as recently Pape, who knew the crossing so singularly well, allows for transit "from two or three hours before low water until three hours before the next high tide, a period of about six hours altogether" thus approving a longish period which provided time for no little margin of error.

Almost certainly the first settlers of the land of Cartmel came across the bay and made the Kirkhead area their place of settlement. As we have seen here there have been found immensely ancient prehistoric relics. Here also was where the Anglians set up the first chapel in the district and here, Wraysholme became the centre of what became the manor of Allithwaite. But it is very likely that the foundation of Cartmel priory changed the main northern terminus of the over-Sands route, though it would, of course, be unwise to assume that at any time all travellers from the Lancaster side of the Bay came ashore at the same point of the Cartmel coast, since once the channel of the Kent had been cleared, access to either the Cart Lane or Kents Bank area was mostly easy enough.

The first obstacle in the Bay which faced the traveller from Lancaster was the channel of the modest little river Keir, but this normally posed no serious problem (it is significant that only in 1820 was it thought advisable to appoint a guide here). The rest of the journey, notably the channel of the Kent was, however potentially dangerous; at an unknown date locals formulated the proverb "Kent and Keir have parted many a good man and his mare".

As we have seen, Cartmel priory was responsible for appointing a guide whose duty it was to conduct over the sands members of the public who so desired. It is quite likely that the monastery established what it found a more convenient place for this northern terminus at Cart Lane, just west of Grange-over-Sands which was connected with their monastery by an excellent dry and reliable road over the hill which, unlike most of the local tracks, could be used by carts in all weathers. This, almost certainly, became the main route from Cartmel to Lancaster. But one or two other tracks met it at the foot of Risedale which were also usable by carts proceeding up or down the lane to the shore long known as Cart Lane. The guide himself came to be sometimes known as the Carter though probably he mostly directed the traffic from his nag. As we have seen the 1535 *Valor Ecclesiasticus* in its valuation of Cartmel priory terms him grandiloquently "bailiff and conductor of all the people of the lord King across the sands of the sea called Cartmel Sands by foundation of the founder". From the first, no doubt, there went along with the guide's pay a house and a little land, whilst he might well expect also tips from grateful travellers. Inevitably local public needs led to the retention of this office at the Reformation. Recently the suppression of this picturesque post with its now far from princely perquisites was monstrously urged by some faceless bureaucrat, happily without success.

As the guide's appointment went to the Crown after the suppression of the priory, the names of its holders after this time can be traced. It seems that from late Elizabethan times to the mid-eighteenth century the post became virtually hereditary in the Carter family. A moment's thought will show that such a monopoly, far from being scandalous was sensible, since the stupendous variation in their conditions made long personal scrutiny of the Sands the only way of safeguarding the public from dangers.

What exactly were the perils which threatened the traveller over Sands? A major one was certainly that of being overtaken and trapped by the incoming tide which, as locals know well, can here flow with enormous speed, specially notable off Grange and Arnside being the "bore", a low wall of water which charges in with immense celerity. It is to be remembered in this connection that during the very great part of the times in which the over-Sands route was in use there were no tide-tables at all and even when they came to be printed only a very small proportion of the travellers possessed them. The best thing to do, it must often have been to hope for the best and arrive at the terminus and then discover from the guide or from the locals what was the next suitable time for crossings, even if this might entail no little waiting.

Another very real menace for men and animals offered by the Sands, the end of which is not yet, came from the quicksands great and small, which the unwary could very easily fail to recognise with results that could easily be fatal, especially for those on horse-back or in vehicles. Tradition tells that some time ago near Arnside after sands there had shifted there was revealed the skeleton of a horse and his rider trapped in this way. Present-day experience shows that once a person has been caught like this, release is almost impossible.

Much the greatest asset of crossing the Sands in company with the Guide was the value of his help in crossing the formidable channel of the river Kent, whose course tended to be unpredictable; an interesting agreement over fishing in the area made between Cartmel priory and the lord of Beetham in the time of King John shows vividly that in those days as in our own, the river was apt to change course dramatically, being sometimes close to the shore at Grange, at others right over on the Westmorland side[5] and also sometimes flowing well between the two. Not only did the river's course change, but it sometimes flowed in a single channel, at others in more, whilst in some parts at times for one reason or another its depth would be found to be very much deeper than was normal. Such changes went on constantly and sometimes rapidly and were liable to be complicated by the changes in the weather so common in these parts. Fog was another menace, and one hard to combat until the age of the pocket compass, though we find coach drivers relying on the often steady wind to check their course in such circumstances. Thus a major duty of

---

[5] A curious result of this inconstancy was that the small island near Grange Station known as Holme Island until very recently was sometimes in Lancashire and at others in Westmorland, since the river Kent (which was the boundary between the two counties) sometimes flowed on one side of it sometimes on the other. This was ended by the vigorous railway engineer Alexander Brogden who, having built himself a desirable residence on the island firmly linked it with Grange and Lancashire by a stout causeway.

the Guide was to explore the Sands for the best passage at any particular time, it becoming usual for him to indicate this for the public benefit with a line of markers which were known as "brobs"; branches of laurel came to be favoured for this purpose, being tough and having leaves which lasted long, even when dry.

We have unfortunately no statistics to show what proportion of the travellers of the Sands lost their lives in the crossing, but almost certainly it was quite small, since, providing reasonable precautions were taken, it was normally safe enough. Local parish registers, not least those of Cartmel and, at a latish date, local newspapers, do however provide details of a not inconsiderable number of losses of life here.

To modern eyes it might seem, at first sight, that our ancestors would have been better advised to go from Lancaster to North Lonsdale and its adjacent areas by land, but contemporaries were very wise in largely neglecting this route unless some special circumstance made it necessary. Of the disadvantages which it involved, that of distance was the most formidable. Green's magnificent *"Tourists' New Guide"* (1819) estimates the distance from Lancaster to Ulverston over Sands to be 21 miles (3 to Hest Bank, another 10 to Cart Lane, $3\frac{1}{2}$ more through Flookburgh to the Leven estuary and $4\frac{1}{2}$ across it to Ulverston) and goes on to assess the total distance from Lancaster to Ulverston by "the nearest road ... to avoid the Sands" which went by Carnforth and Heversham to Levens and on via Lindale, Newton and Newby Bridge at 38 miles. An attractive stone in the wall at Causeway End, Cartmel still informs the public that the distance "over Sands" to Lancaster is 15 miles, to Ulverston 7.

This meant in practise that whereas the journey from Lancaster to Ulverston over the Sands could easily be done in a day, even by pedestrians (who in these parts tend to be tough), the route over land by Beetham and Levens would take even a horseman a very long while over difficult and desolate ground by no means well provided with hostelries. But the over-Sands route was clearly apt to be time-wasting, especially for those coming or going to Furness, since these would also have to cross the smallish but perilous Leven estuary (see p. 45). In this connection it is worthy of note that those who could do so provided themselves with hostels where food and shelter could be acquired. Furness abbey, Cartmel priory, Lancaster priory and Cockersand abbey all had properties in or near Bolton-le-Sands and Hest Bank which are likely to have been employed for this, whilst Furness abbey had at Kents Bank what was probably largely a hostel that came to be known as Abbot Hall (see p. 68). At Wraysholme was a hall owned by the Harringtons which must have been a useful stopping place for its owners and their household. At Conishead priory itself almost certainly no little hospitality was extended to travellers from the nearby route across the Leven estuary. Most of these arrangements were, of course, largely nullified by the suppression of the monasteries, though the considerable need for the facilities which they offered only disappeared with the advent of the railways.

Although history has unhappily denied us the delight of having films of those over Sands crossings, some of which were certainly picturesque, early guidebooks and other sources, such as the invaluable *Lonsdale Magazine*, provide us with lively accounts of the passage. A writer in the 1820 number of the latter tells how his journey began at 5 a.m. when his coach-driver burst unceremoniously into his room in a Lancaster hotel exclaiming "For God's sake make haste... The tide is down... if you delay we shall all be drowned". When the main channel was reached "there could not be fewer than forty carts, gigs, horse-chaises, etc. with men, women, children, dogs and I can hardly tell what besides all in the river at once.... It would have been a fine model to draw the Passage of the Red Sea from". Waves splashed through wheels and horses were breast-deep in water. Cocklers were met on the uneventful journey which terminated at Kent's Bank where there was "a solitary inn by the sandside", the traveller pushing on via "the more circuitous route through Flookburgh".

Thirty years later – in 1850 – a writer crossing in the opposite direction noted "Sometimes the number of people and conveyances which cross from hence to Hest Bank on the opposite shore, is so great as to present the appearance of a caravan traversing the Arabian desert, but consisting of oxen, sheep, horsemen, fishermen, carriers, chaises, gigs, coaches, all in close succession, instead of the dromedaries and turbaned inhabitants of the East". He notes "a few yards errors may pitch the coach, when crossing the waters of the channel, into a deep gulf made by the shifting sand" but had total confidence in the coachman who confided "We drives by the wind, sur, in the mist and in the dark... I know as how it does not change much". In Leigh's *Guide to the Lakes and Mountains of Cumberland, Westmorland and Lancashire* (3rd edn. 1835) it is noted *inter alia* that "the guide at the Keir is on foot and at the Kent on horseback.... On a fine day nothing can be more delightful than a ride over the Lancaster Sands" and in this opinion it was not alone.

This over-Sands route was in itself picturesque and gave access to some truly magnificent scenery so that it is not surprising that it attracted no little attention from the artists who from the late eighteenth century onwards so often came to the Lakes to perpetuate its beauties by their brushes. Turner's elaborate picture of the coach and various pedestrians reaching the Lancaster end of the over-Sands route (Pl. 7a) has very often been reproduced. Less well known but in some ways more interesting is David Cox's "Lancaster Sands" (Pl. 6a). This shows the Sand gleaming wet with the puddles left by the ebbing tide. In the foreground is the guide from Cart Lane on his nag, who is explaining the route which the day's conditions demand to the leaders of the miscellaneous straggling travellers that have met him.

The Leven Estuary

Travellers seeking Furness or South Cumberland had a further estuary to cross after treading Cartmel soil – the smallish but rather perilous one of the powerful Leven which flowed out of Windermere, whose waters were reinforced by those of the river Crake which flows mildly down from Coniston. This crossing was west of Flookburgh, and there seems to have been more than one route to it from the Kents Bank area, including one on the higher ground which for obvious reasons was used by coaches. The road from Flookburgh to the crossing point was known as Sandgate (the second element of this word, as is usual in Scandinavian areas, meaning "road" not "gate" in the modern sense) and ran over firm ground not to be found further south. The opposite coast of Furness was usually very visible, being a bare three miles away. The comparatively short crossing here was virtually intersected by a small but sturdy island for whose existence scores of travellers down the ages must have thanked God, as it offered refuge for those who for one reason or another were in danger of losing their lives on the sands nearby. It has long been known as Chapel Island, though its ancient name was Harlsyde; probably in late medieval times it acquired a small chantry chapel to which no contemporary reference is known.

Beyond, the traveller joined the land route into Furness close to the priory of Conishead. This establishment originated about 1190 as a small house of Austin canons, and offered hospitality to travellers and infirm, but became a domestic residence after the dissolution of the monasteries, the place being rebuilt on a stupendous scale by Colonel Thomas Richmond Gale Braddyll who ruined the family fortunes thereby. He also erected on Chapel Island the enormous piece of gabled walling with lancet windows which is very visible from afar, but is as bogus as the hermitage which he erected in his grounds, with a hermit (who was equally bogus and under contract not to cut his hair or nails!). There are to be seen on Chapel Island some slight remains of what may well be the medieval chapel cheek by jowl with the unlovely remnants of a (?) nineteenth-century fisherman's hut.

Just as Cartmel priory had the responsibility of appointing and paying an official guide for the public over the Sands of Kent and Keir, so Conishead priory had the same duty for the Levens estuary. The *Valor Ecclesiasticus* of 1535 records that this house paid an annual salary of 66s. 8d. to John Hartley "bailiff and conductor of all the people of the lord King over the sands of the sea called Kent Sands" (this latter title being certainly erroneous). His office also still remains, the guide's house being on the Furness coast near the Ulverston canal. Although the journey across these Sands was so short it was known to be far from immune from peril. Some annals of Furness abbey tell us that Michael de Furness, lord of Aldingham was drowned here whilst returning from a visit to Cartmel in 1269. Had he prayed too long or feasted too much?

Two worthy witnesses give very different estimates of the value of this over-Sands route. The shrewd old Thomas West who knew the area so well wrote in 1774 "The approach to Furness . . . from Lancaster hath always been considered as dangerous: but it is less so now than formerly, the sands being more solid; and in company with guides few accidents happen . . . . The river Kent hath its channel, and a guide on horseback is always in waiting to conduct travellers over at the stated hours . . . . The Leven sands are safe, yet the ford, like that of the Kent, is frequently changing by the shifting of the sands. This ford is every day tried by the guide, and in his company you are safe".

Fifteen years earlier John Wesley, the greatest traveller of his age to come this way, failed to find the journey to his liking. On 11 May 1759 at a time when locals asserted to be too late to cross, he left Lancaster, "passed the seven-mile sand to Fluckborough" and went on to "cross the Millam-Sand without either guide or difficulty, to Bottle twenty-four measured miles from Fluckborough then on to Whitehaven over the ford at Muncaster". "I have taken my leave of the sand road" he writes. "I believe that it is ten measured miles shorter than the other, but there are four sands to pass, so far from each other, that it scarce is possible to pass them all in one day; especially as you have all the way to do with a generation of liars, who detain all strangers as long as they can, for their own gain or their neighbours. I can advise no stranger to go this way; he may go round by Kendal and Keswick, often in less time, always with less expense, and far less trial of his patience". Can it be that he lacked the Lakeland penchant for hastening slowly?

Literary figures too passed this way. It was in the neighbourhood of Chapel Island that Wordsworth received with rapturous delight news of the death of Robespierre, as he relates in *The Prelude* which tells incidentally of

>a dilapidated structure, once
>A Romish chapel, where the vested priest
>Said matins at the hour that suited those
>Who crossed the sands with ebb of morning tide.
>Not far from that still ruin all the plain
>Lay spotted with a variegated crowd
>Of vehicles and travellers, horse and foot
>Wading beneath the conduct of their guide.

When in 1830, Mrs Felicia Hemans came north to worship the great Wordsworth she came across the Leven sands, as she relates in a letter of 22 June of this year – "I must not forget to tell you that he (Wordsworth) not only admired our exploit in crossing the Ulverston sands as a deed of "derring do", but as a decided proof of taste; the Lake scenery, he says, is never seen to such advantage as after the passage of what he calls its majestic barrier".

Roads and Turnpikes

From Anglo-Saxon days down to the opening phases of the Industrial Revolution English roads were mostly in a most deplorable condition, and there is little doubt that those of north-western England were a good deal worse than most, partly because of the poverty of the area, but principally life here was very largely local and agricultural with most communities largely supplying their own modest needs, and no major English routes traversing the area. In 1770 Arthur Young, one of the busiest travellers of the age, wrote of Lancashire "let me most seriously caution all travellers who may accidentally propose to travel this terrible country to avoid it as they would the devil, for a thousand to one they will break their necks or their limbs by overthrows or breaking down" and in 1796 another writes in similar vein – "avoid Lancashire roads if you value your bones they are all bad and the turnpike roads are no better than the rest". How true this was may be glimpsed from Stockdale's description of a return journey from Ulverston to Cark which he made with his parents in their gig in 1810. Their outward trip had been quickly and easily made across the Sands, but the flooding tide made the return back the same way impossible for several hours. So the party decided to drive home by way of Pennybridge and Bigland (there was no good road to Cark across the Mosses at this time) a distance of fifteen miles. In the event the journey took them no less than three and a half hours because of "rough roads, wooden bridges and precipitous hills"; the important bridge across the Leven had to be carefully tested before use for the presence of holes and decayed planks!

From the early decades of the eighteenth century the construction of turnpikes – carefully constructed lengths of road for the use of which a fee was levied – got under way, but understandably tended to concentrate on routes likely to be lucrative such as the great road north from Lancaster to Carlisle. So far as North Lonsdale was concerned very understandably progress in this sphere was very slow, since the route over the Sands, however infuriating its dependence on the time-table, was by no means unsatisfactory and largely satisfied the modest needs of the local population. The first major step here came quite late, the construction of an excellent through road from Levens to Lindale, on to Newton and Newby Bridge. The Act authorising this was passed in 1818, and made intelligent use of existing strips of road. The invaluable Green, writing in 1819 notes that "the intended new road..., now in great forwardness, is intended to be completed in half a year from the present time". Three years later the *Lonsdale Magazine* rapturously acclaims the finished work, noting amongst other things, how greatly it had swelled the traffic to Newby Bridge.

Modes of Travel

There is little doubt that the amount of wheeled traffic in our area was very small indeed in the long centuries before the advent of the railway and the motorcar. The most obvious form of transport was the cart or wagon but there is evidence to suggest that use of these was far rarer in Lakeland than in many other parts of the country. Writing as late as 1789 Clarke notes that "not above twenty years ago any kind of wheel carriage was totally unknown in Borrodale.... In carrying home their hay (for they make no stacks) they (the locals) lay it upon their horses in bundles, one on each side" – manure and other goods were transported in similar wise. There is no reason to believe this usage was unique. Bad roads, and the rapidly changing weather which so often made speed in gathering hay and harvest a most vital necessity in our region, were two of the main factors which probably explain why in our area so many farms had barns not centralised in their own farmyard but scattered about their land. Certainly these tubby little barns are very numerous indeed, not least in Cartmel, and would make transport of crops thereto a speedy and simple matter. Carts, of course, there were, though when they became widely used we do not know. It is very likely that in Cartmel for long their iron-bound wheels were mostly manufactured in or near the old smithy situated north of the priory gatehouse, and which only comparatively recently relinquished this traditional function. In the writer's childhood wheels with their newly-made rims were still being pushed down the small slope adjoining the smithy into the beck to cool; because of this the near-by bridge (which in medieval times led to a private entrance to monastic grounds) came to be known as Wheel-house bridge, though here, of course, it was horse-shoeing which provided most of the trade. As we have seen, carts from Cartmel priory to Kents Bank joined others to continue to the sea down Cart Lane which was certainly the major local route for wheeled traffic in our area – hence its name. Down the ages hundreds of local folk must have used it for transport to and from the town of Lancaster, which for so very long provided a variety of facilities not to be found in North Lonsdale. Wagons, used to carry goods for the public in our area, have a late and very obscure history.

Very few indeed were the local individuals whose income allowed them the immense luxury (if such it were in ancient days) of travelling there by coach, a thing largely unknown before the eighteenth century in these parts. An early and very rare example of this is found in 1727 when James Lowther, whose family was already at this time almost certainly the wealthiest in Lakeland, decided to travel thus through Furness, though it was feared that his coach would be "rather too broad for those narrow roads". Some fifty years later Lord George Cavendish used a similar conveyance in his travel from southern parts to Holker Hall, but the state of the Cartmel roads rendered it necessary to park it before he got there and attain his residence by less exalted means.

A notable if limited advance came with the introduction of that most picturesque of all forms of Western transport – the coach and horses. As far as is known at present, the first example of this to be seen in North Lonsdale was a diligence or chaise which carried three persons and plied over Sands, between the King's Arms at Ulverston and the Sun Inn at Lancaster. It is first mentioned in the *Cumberland Pacquet* of 11 September 1781 and ran at times permitted by the tide daily except Sundays, the return trip being made on alternate days. Stockdale tells us that for some years until about 1800 long coaches called "dillies" which held thirteen passengers inside and "a heavy load of luggage passengers on the top" were in use on this route and passed to Sandgate via the main street at Flookburgh, three or four running daily. But their considerable weight meant them fairly easily being trapped by quicksands, so they were replaced by smaller and lighter vehicles which reached the shore by Cark, not by Flookburgh. Faringdon writing in 1816 notes that "coaches go also to Ulverstone after every tide across the Ulverstone sands" (Pl. 6b).

However, wheeled traffic certainly played a very minor part in Lakeland history down to Victorian times. For the transport of goods much more important was the pack-horse, with panniers athwart its back, which for centuries largely unaided fulfilled an invaluable function. The heaviness of the animals' loads meant that the pack-horse tracks (of which no few still cross the mountains and fells of Lakeland) follow the contours of the slopes as far as possible and when they go uphill do so in very gentle fashion. As they were easily the dominant form of transport and needed very little space, these roads were mostly only a very few feet wide and the same is true of their bridges of which some noble examples yet remain, though far too many have disappeared. It is claimed that the use of pack-horses in Lakeland finished completely only in 1870.

The poorness of so much of the land of our area meant that horses were comparatively few in number on farms both great and small, a factor which must have done much to develop that readiness to walk long distances, which until very recently was a marked feature of Lakeland life and was not entirely extinct, even in quite recent times. When the new hall at Grisedale was being built in the first years of this century, one of the workmen there involved, walked there and back daily to his labours – a total distance of some 10 miles. Work began at 6 a.m. and ended at 6 p.m., his pay of 18s. a week being expected to support a family of seven. Just after World War II, when the site of the ancient church at Flookburgh was being demolished, another workman living at Backbarrow engaged on this, walked to and from work (a total distance of some dozen miles), as well as working a long day. Various instances of local men walking to London can be found, but in general such ventures to alien parts were probably viewed with suspicion; on the glass of one light of a window in Cartmel Fell Church, a (? sixteenth century) local has daubed the note "Wilm Brigg goeth to London upon Tusday xij[th] day of Aprill. God save hym".

The Coming of the Railway

Although, as we shall see, Geography and Geology in their mercy prevented the rural peace of Cartmel being at all seriously menaced by industrialism, very early in the history of this major revolution it looked briefly as if the land might find itself traversed by nothing less prestigious than the main western railroad from London to Scotland. Such a line was obviously a major objective once railways were seen to be feasible propositions, and a plan for this in the area was initiated as early as 1836, for the Maryport and Carlisle Railway, to link it with Lancaster and provide what would be a level line up to Scotland, which, of course, was a thing not to be had further inland because of the mountains and hills of Lakeland.

After surveying the area with this in view in August 1837 the great George Stephenson strongly and speedily backed the idea. He proposed to route the line from Lancaster to Poulton and thence across the Sands to Humphrey Head, on from here to Chapel Island through Lindal Moor by a tunnel at Kirkby Ireleth to Whitehaven. An important feature of the scheme was its proposal to reclaim a large and, as it was believed, profitable area of the bay. However the following year a body terming itself the Provisional Committee of the Caledonian, West Cumberland and Furness Railway commissioned one John Hague, another engineer skilled in such matters, to investigate. His report selected a route from Poulton which by-passed Cartmel and crossed the Furness coast-line at Leonard Point, some 3 miles N.E. of Rampside; he calculated that this could make feasible the reclamation of 46,300 acres of Morecambe Bay whose sale would be highly profitable.

By this time very understandably other districts had very different ideas about the siting of this important route. One scheme proposed that it go by Kendal and Long Sleddale, through a tunnel to Haweswater, Penrith and on to Carlisle, another up the Lune valley on to Tebay, Crosby Ravensworth, Penrith and Carlisle. A government Commission to consider the rival schemes was set up in August 1839 and quickly plumped for the Lune route, ruling out the coastal one as too long and to expensive. Cartmel's chance of being on or near a main route to Scotland had gone for ever, but its inhabitants cannot be said to have suffered any significant loss as a result.

However the railways of Furness steadily became very important. The principal reason for this was the vigorous and skilful exploitation of the slate quarries of Kirkby in Furness and the prolific and high quality iron ore of Lindal and Dalton. In 1856 more than 500,000 tons of the latter was shipped from Barrow-in-Furness and three years later Messrs Schneider and Hannay gave an immense industrial boost to the area by establishing iron works which developed into the steel works and blast furnaces of the Barrow Haematite Steel Company. In 1873 came another most important development – the establishment of the Barrow Ship-Building Company which finally became the mighty firm of Vickers Ltd.

This immense industrial progress in Furness not only led to the rapid transmutation of what early in the century had been the tiny village of Barrow into a town of very substantial size, but also boosted enormously the power of the Furness Railway. This had begun in humble fashion in 1843-6 originally running only from Kirkby to Roa Island and Piel Pier with a branch to Lindal, with passengers accommodated in a sheep van, but quickly expanded in a variety of ways, including provisions for visits to Furness abbey from Fleetwood and construction of an almost totally useless line to Conishead (whose history is as near nil as makes no matter) as well as the takeover of various small local lines and the construction of docks. Between 1793 and 1876 no less than 35 private Acts of Parliament relating to the Furness Railway were passed.

Odd as it now seems, establishment of rail contact between North Lonsdale and the great Lancaster to Carlisle lines for long was not regarded as a high priority, principally, no doubt, because very good facilities for transport by sea could be and were quickly developed at Barrow, and also because of the considerable costs and difficulties involved in constructing a line across the Leven and Kent estuaries. The earliest proposal to link up with the main Carlisle line was made by the Whitehaven and Furness Junction Committee in 1845 but was still-born. Success came largely through the vigour and initiative of the Brogden family of Manchester which had Ulverston connections, and in 1851 established the Ulverston and Lancashire Company to this end. The line they constructed from Ulverston did not go beyond Carnforth, where it connected with the Lancaster and Carlisle Railway (which was destined to be swallowed up by the London and North-Western Railway). The task of construction of this line was more than usually difficult, involving not only the bridging of the estuaries of Leven and Kent but the construction of a considerable amount of highly expensive embankment. The small Company's lack of capital made it dependent on the help of the powerful Furness Railway from which, amongst other things, it hired its locomotives. The first viaducts were made of wood and the line came into use in 1857 with stations at Cark, Kents Bank, Grange-over-Sands, Arnside and Silverdale.

The first of these acquired the title of "Cark and Cartmel", perhaps to attract tourists but if so it was a move which seems to have had no significant success. The station itself served Holker Hall where lived the Duke of Devonshire who played so vigorous and valuable a part in developing the industry of Furness, and was given special treatment. The entrance to the station from the village of Cark was by a broad avenue bounded by copses well supplied with shrubs, and Cark alone of the five stations had a substantial iron bridge for the use of travellers crossing the line and a quite elaborate waiting room for top people. The platforms had the special Furness railway seats (now very much collectors' pieces) with their fine cast-iron bench ends which, *inter alia*, displayed a squirrel eating nuts. The station-master paraded in a fine frock-coat adorned with special Furness Railway buttons. In accordance with normal Victorian practice, express trains could be stopped specially for Holker Hall passengers since originally its owner had allowed the line to be built over no little of his property. For this facility there was a special stopping place at the crossing west of Cark station. A familiar sight on the Cark platform down to the outbreak of World War II were the sacks of shellfish now despatched afar by Flookburgh fishermen (see p. 62). In 1860 the Company planned to erect at Cark its own workshop.

Kents Bank was small since it served only a smallish local population, though the conversion of Abbot Hall into a holiday home (1915) boosted its intake. Grange-over-Sands, on the contrary, was part and parcel of a major attempt to boost the place as a tourist centre (see p. 93) and was given a long platform with attractive roofing and biggish offices. The land on both sides of it was so low and irregular that a considerable amount of what must have been expensive embankment was needed in this area, and no little beautification of the land on the north side of the station was undertaken, which may well have buried very deep indeed some useful archaeological information. The Ulverston and Lancaster Company was from the first living on minor financial resources and even the establishment of the boost to its resources given by Schneider and Hannay's blast furnaces was inadequate to maintain its independence. In 1862 it was bought out by the Furness Railway, which was now well on the way to prosperity.

In 1876 was added a very attractive little line from Grange to Kendal, long faithfully served by an engine known as "Kendal Tommy". Making no unnecessary noise and emitting no excessive smoke on his pleasing route, he was never overworked and could often be seen in contemplative mood in a siding at Grange; his demise was much regretted by many. Meanwhile a steamer service on Windermere had been begun in 1871, being linked by rail with Ulverston and Plumpton. Even earlier – in 1859 – a most elegant steam gondola ("the Lady of the Lake") began to delight tourists on Coniston lake; after a long period of neglect she has been most enterprisingly and magnificently restored to life, and in 1980 went in to action again.

For Cartmel itself the advent of the railways clearly made travelling to and from the area much easier and largely eliminated its ancient use of the old routes.[6] It allowed easier sale of stock, an auction mart (recently destroyed) being built at Cark, and obviously boosted tourism though this was not on a very large scale. But

Plate 7a — Lancaster Sands by J. M. W. Turner *(The British Museum)*.

Plate 7b — Cartmel Fell Church.

Plate 8 — Cartmel Fell Church.

a. The Crucifix.

Stained Glass:
    b. Ordination.
    c. Mass.

there was mercifully no great industrial activity in the land of Cartmel and in our own day, no small part of the rail traffic which traversed it, notably that of frequent and heavy goods trains rumbling between Barrow and the great outside world is now no more.

[6] Passenger traffic across the Leven sands quickly slumped to a very small number of folk, most of whom were tramps unable to afford the train fare. At one stage the guide here gave their fare to individual gentlemen of the road to spare himself the journey, but news of this quickly spread and tramps became very numerous. As a result the guide decided to buy himself a horse and, when one of the fraternity turned up, he expressed willingness to conduct him over Sands as he was legally required to do, but added ominously "I ride, you walk", thus killing off a source of easy money.

CHAPTER FIVE

MATTERS ECONOMIC

IN view of the importance of the economic factor in history, it is essential to give it some consideration here, though for various reasons this must be somewhat brief. Cartmel possessed no substantial natural resources to exploit for great profit. Its iron supply, at least after medieval times, was very insignificant and its slate quarries (at Newton) even more so. Further, nowhere did its coastline provide a site for a sizeable port, the little harbour at Grange being quite useless in the industrial age. Of the two major factories established in the area – the cotton mill at Backbarrow and the great corn mill at Cark – both quite quickly collapsed, for a variety of reasons. It is further to be noted that documentary evidence of economic activity in Cartmel is remarkably sparse. We have no accounts of the cotton mill at Cark or of the factory at Lowwood, whilst of the cloth trade and shipping which formerly existed, evidence, both historical and archaeological, is meagre in the extreme.

The Iron Trade

The only industry in medieval Cartmel which was of the slightest interest to the outside world was its iron trade. As we have seen, the possibility of iron mines being developed here is to be found in the foundation charter of Cartmel priory about 1190 and this almost certainly became a reality quite soon. We have next to no documentary evidence on the course of its history, though the fourteenth century account rolls of Bolton priory show us that this house was then purchasing iron from Cartmel. This suggests some fairly large deposits which were quite possibly in the region of Pit Farm, whose name may derive from workings left behind by the miners. But we have no signs of iron-working at Cartmel for a very long while after this, though in the seventeenth century it seems to have taken on a limited new lease of life with local gentry speculating therein, albeit apparently without any great success. A forge existed by 1685 in Cark Shaws wood, owned originally by Thomas Preston who later went into partnership with James Machell for making iron here but this venture ceased before 1711.

In Cartmel, only one place was of importance in the history of local iron-trade in the days of the Industrial Revolution. This was Wilson House, just outside Lindale, where important work was begun, developed by two men – Isaac Wilkinson, a Cumbrian who had been working in the trade elsewhere for some time (in 1735 he had undertaken to cast iron ware at Backbarrow and Leighton furnace) and patented a flat iron in 1738, and his son John (Pl. 10b), a very vigorous and colourful person, memory of whom is not yet dead in the Lindale area. After working at Backbarrow – a major centre of the local iron industry – they moved to Wilson House where they worked a furnace which they sought to heat by peat, which, it is said, was transported to the furnace on a canal they cut through the moss, by an iron boat which made a great sensation in the area as being the first of its kind, memory of which is still not dead amongst locals. But their work here was no success and John moved off elsewhere to become "the great iron master", owning large ironworks in Shropshire, Staffordshire and Wales. Never troubled by spasms of modesty John Wilkinson excited very considerable criticism by one act. Like no few other businessmen in these times he issued his own trade tokens, but, unlike them, he had put on them his own head, hereby breaking the long established rule that on coinage the only head to be used should be that of the monarch. Like so many folk bred in these parts, love of it never left him, and in 1795 he bought Castlehead, erecting a large house and making a fine garden there. He died in 1808 and arranged to be buried in these grounds. But as we shall see, laying mortal remains to rest proved a surprisingly difficult task (see p. 94). Happily the massive memorial column which he had made for himself yet survives to keep alive the memory of one of Cartmel's most entertaining characters.

It is not unlikely that a fair number of unrecorded minor efforts to mine iron in our area were made from time to time including, possibly, exploration of land across the road from Pit Farm. What was perhaps the last of these efforts came barely a century ago, when in 1870-6 Barrow Haematite Steel Co. thought it worth-while to arrange to seek for it in land attached to Cark Hall. But it seems clear that in Cartmel iron simply did not exist in quantities worthy of commercial exploitation.

Mills

The mills of Cartmel were quite numerous and varied greatly in both their age and their purpose. In medieval times all or most of them were mills made to grind the cereals which loomed so very large in the menus of the people of those days, though in the process of time some of these were put to other uses. Until less than two centuries ago most mills were worked by water wheels, so their distribution is very limited. The river Leven provided much the most powerful and dependable source of water in Cartmel, second being the much smaller Ay, though this from time to time tended to dry up.

Unfortunately we have nothing or next to nothing to help us to ascertain the age of most of these mills. Aynsome mill was an important one and almost certainly was made by the brethren of Cartmel priory at the time of its foundation (the present building is largely modern but high up in one of its walls may yet be seen a stone carved with thirteenth century dog tooth), a special water-course being made to feed it, with fishponds (recently re-discovered) in attendance. A few hundred yards above Walton Hall, where a small beck behind Howbarrow unexpectedly switches course to become a water-fall, was a mill known as Hill Mill which is probably the one termed Holker Mill in some documents. It certainly existed in Elizabethan times and may be much older than this. It was probably rebuilt about the same time as the cotton mill at Cark was erected about 1785, as its architecture looked much the same. It was left untenanted in the last years of the last century and gradually fell into ruin, the very minor remains still visible in recent years disappearing when the nearby residence was built (1979). The mill at Allithwaite is likely to be very old, though little is known of its history; our knowledge of the minor mills at Lindale and Ayside is at least equally obscure.

Much of the most interesting and important mills in Cartmel are the two which formerly existed at Cark,[7] neither of which originated as corn mills. The older of these which came to be known as the Little Mill was apparently one of the oldest paper mills in England. A special water course was created for it, fed by water diverted from the main stream of the Ay which ran from a point some three hundred yards north of Cark Hall southward in what was very nearly a straight line, passing only a few yards from the garden in front of the Hall to create a useful fall of water into the main stream of the Ay below Tenter Bank at Cark. In the parish registers of Cartmel Church occur references to two of the earliest workers at the Mill. In March 1617 was christened there "Jenett Sauell dau: of Francis labore at the paper milne" and in October 1621 "Marye Sceauell dau: of Francis of Nether Carke paper man", whilst in March 1621 was buried "Thomas Higgins paperman". The name of the father of Jenett and Mary is obviously a very unusual one, suggesting he was certainly "from off", as we say. Could he have been a foreigner? There is no doubt that the mill itself was built *de novo*.

One is bound to ask why this very rare type of mill was found at so very early a date at so singularly remote a place as Cark which, in the early seventeenth century consisted of very little beyond the newly-constructed hall, a minor handful of houses, and a small creek. It is the opinion of the present writer (which it is unlikely that concrete evidence in adequate quantity will ever be found to either confirm or deny) that the answer to this question is to be found in the fact that Cartmel and Furness area at this time was largely in the hands of gentry who were "church papists" (George Preston of Holker, as we have seen, was for long nominally Anglican but died in 1640 as a Roman Catholic). The very remoteness of Cark, coupled with its creek made it a very suitable place both in which to make paper for the papist writings that were now forbidden by the law of the land, and to smuggle it away, without much fear of detection by the government officials on the Lancaster side of the Bay.

After George Preston's time the owners of the Holker estates were Anglican; we find them leasing out the paper mill, Thomas Preston in Feb. 1660, Sir William Lowther in Dec. 1704 and Sir Thomas Lowther in 1723. By 1734 the place had apparently become a hemp mill, but in 1835 it was a paper mill again. Probably soon after it became a small corn mill, and so remained for about a century. Very recently the place has been converted into attractive domestic accommodation and the watercourse which fed it is now filled in or dry.

[7] A collection of early deeds concerning them has been deposited in the Record Office at Barrow by the present writer, but has not yet been fully studied.

Although the history of the Little Mill at Cark is unspectacular, the same is not true of the huge "Big Mill" (Pl. 15b) and it is most fortunate that the survival of various of its early deeds enable us to clarify and extend Stockdale's account of it. It was established by a group of five men whose legal agreement to do this is dated 9 May 1785 – they were John Ryder of Manchester merchant, Joseph Thackeray of Manchester merchant, Thomas Satterthwaite of Lancaster merchant, James Stockdale of Cark merchant and, rather surprisingly, Edward Hardy of Cark cabinet maker. The agreement was for 20 years dated from the previous 1st January and the aim was "the business of buying, spinning and manufacturing and selling of cotton" at Cark where, this agreement notes, "a certain cotton mill and divers dwelling houses, warehouses and other necessary buildings, have been erected and made".

The expense of acquiring the very large amount of land which this venture necessitated and of erecting the enormous building and its satellite edifices must clearly have been stupendous. It seems likely that the venture involved the take-over not only of a small forge (about whose site we know nothing) but also of the fulling mill and its appurtenances (see p. 61). But expense seems not to have worried the directors, who quickly splashed out also on acquiring one of the very new engines just available to boost their water supply. This "fire engine", as it was termed, caused no little local sensation partly by its novelty and also the noise it made, which, according to Stockdale, could on occasion, be heard at Newton!

Research by Dr W. K. Chaloner has brought out an interesting episode in its history. This engine was, in the words of Stockdale "a pumping engine... and was used for the purpose of lifting the water out of the tail race back into the mill dam, and thus, as it was thought, of ensuring a continuous supply". The pioneers in the field of inventing such a thing was the famous firm of Boulton and Watt who produced and patented a very competent design and in Jan. 1786 James Stockdale (grandfather of his name-sake who wrote "The Annals of Cartmel") and his partners signed a contract for one with this company. But there was delay over the installation which caused the directors great concern at Cark, especially since towards the end of April 1789 as one of them wrote "the dry weather has made us so scarce in water that we have not (enough) to work with half the time". In July another wrote urgently "we have not less than upwards of 400 people nearly unemployed and not one fourth of their time at work". A slightly later letter (1790) shows that the mill had 3400 spindles of which the water power supplied by the steam engine could drive 1200 or about a third.

Trouble flared up when the Cark directors tried a second and finally a third engine. The latter began to work in 1794, but its design infringed Boulton and Watts patent, so the latter firm sent an industrial spy to collect proof of this transgression with the aid of the Cark workers, which he was able to do "with the assistance of half-crown pieces... this I found enough for any Engine man". Appropriately he stayed at what was then the Fire Engine Inn. On 2 May 1796 a legal injunction stopped the Cark engine and after arbitration the Cark company had to pay Messrs Boulton and Watt £550 damages. Stockdale tells us that the smoke of the "fire engine" was directed to a chimney erected at some little distance from the mill so that it would not blacken the wall of the mill. This chimney stood some halfway between the mill and the gatehouse to it, but was demolished before the mill itself was destroyed: what may be part of the engine itself still exists.

There can be little doubt that the establishment of the Big Mill and its attendant structures involved *inter alia* major reconstruction of no small part of the village. The prolongation of the water-course below the Little Mill and the creation of a dam for it to fill was an early move, and provided water for the massive water wheel which survived until the fire of 1936, and whose shaft was said, almost certainly correctly, to have been made by John Wilkinson. The great mill itself was an enormous building of five storeys with a large yard on its southern side flanked with a row of cottages on either side. Entrance was by an attractive little gatehouse with a single room at first floor level entered by a small flight of stone steps and guarded by an iron bound door. At this time the course of the Ay which flanked it was probably straightened out and its southern bank built up to its present high level, whilst the Fire Engine Inn (now the Engine Inn) must belong at least largely if not wholly to this time. A tail race was constructed under the mill. To the west and north of the mill were built three rows of cottages (see p. 78).

It is unfortunate that none of the business papers of this mill are known to have survived, and that, so far, no evidence to show us the precise date at which the cotton venture which it housed collapsed, as it certainly did some time before 1850. In the latter part of the century it was used as a corn-mill, a purpose for which it was far too large, and this continued until its destruction by fire in 1936.

The river Ay with its very modest water supply could not expect to run major mills. Exactly opposite was the position of the river Leven. Here no small volume of water came down from Windermere Lake and after coursing through a quite narrow and rocky channel at Backbarrow, crashed over some massive rocks to give a considerable fall of water without any help from engineers. On the right bank of the river just below the fall developed an iron and steel work of major importance established by the Machell and Sandys families in 1710-11, which has remains of considerable interest to the industrial archaeologists, but is situate in Furness, so does not concern us here.

On the Cartmel side of the river at the point where originally was a quite considerable waterfall, at an unknown date Cartmel priory had established a corn mill to which reference is made in a deed of 1565, and was "at or near Backbarrow bridge" as a later document puts in. But by 1790 we have mention of three merchants John Birch, Robert Robinson and William Walmesley (all of whom resided at Broughton Lodge, which, one may presume, they had had constructed, for it belongs to about this time) concerned in jointly carrying on the business of "carding, roving and spinning" at Backbarrow. A notice advertising it for sale or to let, dated 6 July 1807, shows it to have been a very large and complex establishment which was being used for "spinning of Cotton, Flax and Tow". It had three mills each four stories high and one of two stories "with three water-wheels and Mill Gear complete", shops for Joiners, Clocksmiths and Blacksmiths with various other offices. Living accommodation included "a large Dwelling-House now used for Apprentices, and capable of conveniently accommodating up to 200", as well as "80 comfortable, substantial dwellings".

Unhappily for its reputation, very early in the century this Backbarrow mill hit the headlines with great force when an official enquiry revealed that it was most scandalously exploiting child labour under the much too easy-going regulations of the time.[8] Before the government Committee investigating the employment of children in "Manufactories" in 1816, appeared amongst others, Mr John Moss who had been in charge of some 150 apprentices at the cotton mill at Backbarrow from Feb. 1815 to Mar. 1815. He testified that there were children, some from London of ages varying from seven to eleven years, others from Liverpool aged between eight and eleven, all of whom were bound to their apprenticeship until they reached the age of twenty-one. They worked all six weekdays from 5 a.until 8 p.m. with half an hour at 7 a.m. for breakfast and another half hour for dinner at 12, but could eat something at work in the afternoon. When lost time had to be made up they worked till 9 or 10 sometimes for three weeks on end. There were no seats in the mill. If the amount of water only sufficed to work one of the two mills, a night shift was added. On Sundays some or all cleaned machinery from 6 a.m. till noon, any not thus involved being sent to church (at Finsthwaite) three miles away. Nightly inspections tended to show that some had run away or were asleep in the mill. Once when the mill had stopped payment, some children were taken in a cart to the sands on the Lancaster road and turned adrift.

No doubt the indignation which this caused at a high level led the management to engage in improving their image, at least visually. In 1843 Jopling mentions it as "an extensive establishment, belonging to the Messrs Ainsworth, for the manufacture of cotton, where, instead of the gloomy looking factory with its tall black chimney and dusky volumes of smoke are ivy-clustered mills, water-falls, a fountain and shrubs and flowers ornamenting each vacant spot". Earlier, in 1833, Baines had noted briefly "an extensive cotton manufactory carried on by Messrs Ainsworth, Catterall and Co". In 1841 Butterworth recorded that it was then employing 314 hands. However in 1856 came a massive fire which destroyed one of the two main buildings; in 1895 *The Lonsdale Magazine* notes that the place had been closed for financial reasons, having been employing about 250 people. In 1889-90 the two mills on the site (known as the North and South Mills) were taken over by a company known as the British Ultramarine Company to manufacture and sell ultramine lime blue, wash blue paste, red oxide of iron, Prussian blue, etc. In 1925 this establishment was taken over by Reckitts (Colours) Ltd who are the present owners.

Gunpowder

To many it will come as a surprise that for some little time Cartmel had a major gun-powder factory, and that there were others in the neighbourhood. This was

---

[8] See J. L. and B. Hammond, *The Town Labourer*, 1760-1832 (1928).

principally because charcoal was an essential ingredient in the manufacture of gunpowder and was much more easy to obtain in our area than in many other parts of England, demanding, as it did, large expanses of open land on which to grow the enormous quantities of young trees from which charcoal was made.[9] Our factory was at Low-wood on the banks of the Leven and was set up there in or about 1796. The site was chosen partly also for its remoteness from centres of population in case of mishap, as well as because charcoal was in good supply here, but also because the river Leven was navigable and tidal up to this point, having a far greater depth in these days than its narrow width might suggest, which enabled barges to ply between the factory and the estuary where their cargo was trans-shipped. Work for long flourished greatly – in 1800 more than 2000 sacks of charcoal were used in 11 months. By 1860 it had 14 mills in operation, built as separate units with races at different levels and placed well apart as safety precautions; the powder was moved in small wagons which, for similar reasons were drawn by horses with copper hooves on small rail tracks. But in 1863 came a mighty explosion which killed six men and was heard as far away as Kendal. After ownership had changed hands several times the firm closed down in 1935.

Of the old factories themselves there are now only a few buildings left, now converted to domestic and other uses. The storage buildings for ammunition were built very stoutly with the slate slabs of the type so prevalent in Ambleside and Keswick. Of those which survive one has been converted into a bungalow.

Wool

Odd though it may seem to those bred in modern England where industrialization has so long ruled supreme, until comparatively recent centuries England was primarily an agricultural country with wool as its major source of wealth (which, of course, is why it long ago became traditional that the official seat of the Lord Chancellor should be on a woolsack). In late medieval times much of this wool was exported to be made up elsewhere but a cloth trade developed with no few ramifications. In north and western England sheep were a prominent element in local farming, and their wool if not of high quality was valued for its warmth and great durability. As is well known, Kendal early became a major centre for the manufacture and trade in its cloth (the "Kendal green" mentioned by Shakespeare) was of sufficient importance to be regulated by the efficient English government.

In our area, where other employments were sparse, much cloth was made in private houses, and was a useful means of augmenting the often very inadequate income of the poor, notably spinsters and widows. Thus the attractive little Sandes hospital in Kendal was founded in 1670 by Thomas Sandes (who "hath saved a

---

[9] The history of the local charcoal industry is of great interest and ought to be written up before the last first-hand knowledge of it in its final phase becomes unobtainable. It involved, amongst other things, the charcoal burners camping for a while alongside their wood supply in picturesque huts, which led at least one small boy, who unexpectedly came across one such group sixty years ago, to remark "I suppose they are Ancient Britons?".

considerable share of his temporal estate by buying and selling of woollen cottons commonly called Kendal cottons") for "eight poor widows to exercise carding, spinning of wool and weaving of raw pieces of cloth for cottons called Kendal cottons", and there must have been hundreds of women in our region similarly engaged for several centuries, about whose activities next to no records have survived.

However we have an invaluable if almost isolated official side-light on the manufacture of cloth in our area mentioning Cartmel in a spelling odd even by south country standards. This is a short Act of Parliament passed in the reign of James I (1603-25) which bears the informative title "An Act for the incouraginge of many poore people in Cumberland and Westmorland and parishes of Carptmeale, Hawkesheade and Broughton in the Countie of Lancaster, to contynue their trade of makinge Cogware, Kendalls, Carptmeales and course Cottons". The text of the Act shows that attempts had been made by "evell disposed persons . . . to make the said Cogware, Kendalls, Carptmeales and course cottons subject to search and have demanded for the same divers severall sommes of money . . . to the great vexation and trouble of the said poore People". It now forbade such efforts to intervene and laid down that people in the areas there designated "shall make the Cogware, Kendalls, course Cottons and Carptmeales . . . in such sort as may best please the buyer". (7 Jas. I c. XVI.)

It is much to be regretted that so very little is at present known about the Cartmel wool trade in the seventeenth century, though there can be little doubt that here, as in the adjoining regions, in the latter half of the period at least, it helped to give the local countryside a very unusual degree of prosperity at this time. A reminder of the wool trade at Cark is Tenter Bank where cloth used to be stretched.

Shipping

There is no doubt that until the rise of Barrow-in-Furness there was no shipping of very great significance in South Cumbria. For long the only recognised port in the area was Piel and this was not of great importance. Nevertheless it is clear that by the end of the eighteenth century there was a good deal of maritime activity at Lancaster and far along the coastline north of it, with Ulverston and Greenodd as key-points (admittedly smallish) herein. The amount of shipbuilding here was a good deal greater than one might expect, but the vessels produced were small, though this did not prevent them carrying on no little trade with very far distant areas. Unhappily the history of this local maritime activity is very badly documented indeed, especially in the case of Cartmel. It would seem that Grange did not figure much herein but Cark Beck did. The indispensable Stockdale tells us "for many years, vessels of the burden of 50 to 200 tons were built at Carke. My grandfather had a ship-building yard there about the middle of the last century. These vessels traded with countries up to the Baltic or with the then British possessions in America and the West Indies". Unhappily we have no contemporary evidence nor any visible remains to show us the area where they were made or where they docked, though this was probably where the railway and its embankment crosses the now diminutive river Ay.

The tombstones and registers of Cartmel church gives us the names of various local mariners, though we know next to nothing of any of them apart from news given by Thomas Court of Flookburgh who served in the Royal Navy during the Seven Years War (1756-63) and kept a brief but quite interesting diary of his voyages during which he saw actions against French ships.

Fishing

Until very recent times the history of fishing in our area is very obscure indeed. If, as seems likely, Flookburgh gets the first element of its name from the flukes (a smallish but tasty flat fish) we have very early proof of its existence which has certainly always centred on Flookburgh, a place which, as we have seen, was on the existing coast until the enclosures of the last century. Until very recently the Flookburgh families were largely engaged in this and their very Scandinavian vocabulary of fishing terms is of great interest to the philologist.

However, as its smallish old houses suggest, there cannot have been much money in Flookburgh in its early centuries, since markets for fish were purely local ones, because of the very poor transport facilities. The coming of the railway was of considerable value to our fishermen and, as the statistics published annually by Nash plainly show, a considerable trade (largely with Lancashire and Yorkshire towns) developed in shell-fish (largely cockles and mussels) sacks of which could be seen crowding the station at Cark, up to World War II. Between 1882 and 1898 the tonnage of fish (mostly cockles) thus despatched annually varied greatly from 743 to 3161 tons but was mostly in the region of one or two thousand tons, and so long continued. The catch varied somewhat in kind; the figures for twelve months in 1902-3 show $741\frac{1}{2}$ tons of cockles, 171 of mussels and $6\frac{3}{4}$ flukes. After World War II came new problems and new developments which fall outside the terms of reference of this book. For reasons which are disputed, the cockle fishing with its curious technique largely disappeared but that in shrimps developed quickly and profitably, whilst noisy tractors displaced the pleasant old horses and carts.

Minor Trades

Of minor trades at this time there is little that can be said. In North Lonsdale as in Westmorland the local oak furniture, consisting largely of chests, court-cupboards and little spice-cupboards was long a notable feature. It is to be noted that the best pieces of these are mostly, though not always, dated, and that of these the huge majority belong to the period between about 1660 and 1715,[10] the quality showing a tendency to fall as time goes on. Unhappily the drain of these to off-comers via auction sales has a long history and shows no signs of abating. Grandfather clocks have for long been a very much beloved feature of the furnishing of houses great and

[10] It is interesting to note that no small fraction of date stones of local houses fall in this same period.

small in our region, partly because so many dwellings were situate very far down from the parish church and its clock. Lists of local clockmakers have been compiled and include a few Cartmel names. A certain John Dickinson (d. 1780) made a number of clocks in the city of Lancaster of which he was freeman, and then a few at Cartmel, about the year 1758, before moving on to Egremont where he continued his trade until claimed by death. Others in our area of whom we have fragmentary mentions were Miles Anderton (?), Backbarrow d. 1806; Emmanuel Burton, Backbarrow 1790-4; Cornelius Clark(e), Ayside 1733-62; Thomas Clark(e), Cartmel Fell 1767-8; William Clark, Cartmel 1767-8; Thomas Knowles, Cartmel 1784; William Lawrence, Cark, 1785-1818; John Wilkinson Marr, Backbarrow 1838; Edward Storey, Ulverston and Cartmel 1842-9; John Wilkinson, Backbarrow c. 1823-38 (Cartmel church had a clock of which there is mention from 1614 onwards).

In 1825, Corry's *History* notes "In the neighbourhood of Cartmel there is a quarry of granulated limestone which is durable for flags and, when polished, is used for tombstones and chimney pieces". A minor but useful trade now virtually extinct was the manufacture of swills — shallow boat-shaped baskets with small gaps at either end to provide handles woven from flat strips of wood, whose demise local gardeners and agriculturists should regret.

Agriculture

There is very little of importance in the history of agriculture in Cartmel. Nature gave the land great beauty but not much fertility, especially at its northern end. Local conditions prevented the growth of much corn in medieval times, so that we found Cartmel priory, like Furness abbey, getting royal licence to import corn from their possessions in Ireland. This shortage was continued down to the end of our period.[11] There are however two other developments one small and one large, which are worthy of note.

The first of these is a series of attempts to reclaim the coastal lands at the south end of the land of Cartmel.[12] Their total effect was not enormous but they altered the coastline notably in one or two areas. A quite small beginning here was an embankment about half a mile long between Holker Hall and Quarry Flat made by Lord George Cavendish in 1781. Next in 1798 came a very extensive and successful enclosure under the Cartmel Enclosure Act of 1796 which reclaimed a substantial area of land stretching from very near Wraysholme Tower across Winder Moor to a point just south of Canon Winder Hall. Exactly ten years later an embankment of this sought to add another large slice to this addition along its southern side, but in 1828 the western half of this embankment was destroyed with the loss of half the

[11] Board of Agriculture returns for the Cartmel area in 1900 show $1195\frac{3}{4}$ acres producing oats, $83\frac{1}{2}$ wheat, $37\frac{1}{4}$ barley, $223\frac{1}{4}$ turnips, $313\frac{1}{2}$ turnips, 178 mangolds, but clover and seed grass mowing $934\frac{1}{2}$, clover and seed grass pastured $967\frac{3}{4}$, permanent grass mowing 2,427, permanent grass pasture 14,546.

[12] On these see W. Rollinson's paper in *Hist. Soc. of Lancs. and Cheshire*, cxv (1963).

reclaimed land. Finally the construction of the railway across the land of Cartmel somewhat accidentally reclaimed two smallish areas of land – one being the Quarry Flat Marsh the other a larger piece of land south of Old Park and two small ones near Kirkhead. The only major gains were thus Winder Moor and East Plain which were useful but not spectacular.

The Enclosure of the Commons

Immensely important throughout most of Cartmel was the extensive enclosure of land here affected under the Act of Parliament of 1796, which effected very radical changes of several kinds. In our area, as in most of the Lake Counties, right down to the end of the eighteenth century, as some prints of the period show very clearly, the landscape looked very different from what it does now. The peaks and upper slopes of the great mountains mostly, of course, looked much the same, but lower down the picture was greatly diverse. No few of the valley bottoms and other low lying land did not present their now familiar neat green look, had few good roads and not many houses. Instead there was much infertility due principally to lack of drainage. Of our area at this time Stockdale writes "in almost every part of Cartmel parish there were then extensive morasses, swamps, pits, ponds, stagnent sheets of water, obstructed streams and much underdrained, or at any rate very ineffectually drained, land. Not only did these mean much land was not being used to the best advantage, but it led to very wide-spread ague among the population". Higher up the slopes of the fells was a great deal of barren often rocky land which, because it was no use either for cultivation and of only limited use for pasture, was often left largely open for stock to wonder over as it willed – hence the frequency in our area of "pounds" for strayed stock, like that at Field Broughton. No little of the limited pasture land, in accordance with old medieval practice, was used in common here, and because of this was badly over-stocked.

What now occurred at Cartmel, as over many parts of England in the eighteenth and early nineteenth century, was an elaborate official enquiry followed by enclosure of much land that was now divided out (very unequally) amongst those with legal claims, great or small, to such common land. In Cartmel the total area affected was very large indeed, thousands of acres of land being involved.

The change was one which was especially favoured by the well-to-do gentry and here, as usual, they led the way to procuring the Act of 1796 "for improving, dividing and enclosing the commons, waste grounds and mosses in the parish of Cartmel". Heavy initial expenditure was herein involved and met by subscriptions of £200 each from Lord Frederick Cavendish, T. M. Machell, James Stockdale, Langdale Sunderland, George Bigland and Jeremiah Dixon. But this considerable sum proving inadequate for the running expenses was supplemented by advances of £800 and £1352 10s. by James Stockdale (grandfather of the author of the *Annals*) who seems to have been singularly well-supplied with this world's goods.

The very necessary but very protracted and elaborate machinery usual in such cases was now set up to determine with great precision what land was to be closed, how it was to be partitioned amongst the locals, and on what terms. Three commissioners from off were appointed and held their first meeting at the Cavendish Arms on 25 July 1796. By the end of the year they had examined claims for shares in the enclosures and approved 802 of them. Their work was long and complex involving immensely detailed investigations. Only on 3 July 1803 did they instruct surveyors to complete a general map of the parish for their final award. Their long and careful work involving various others was inevitably highly expensive, involving not only payments to officials but making drains, embankments and roads etc. the grand total of the cost coming to £16,914. 16s. 6d. to meet which, considerable portions of the common lands were sold to a value of £18,487. 5s. 5¾d., the principal purchasers being John and Jacob Wakefield of Kendal (£2,500), James Stockdale of Cark (£2,100. 10s. 0d.) and John Wilkinson of Castlehead (£1,880). Amongst their labours, the Commissioners drew up an invaluable list of roads, great and small, in the land of Cartmel (printed in full by Stockdale); at the same time John Wilkinson's brother, William, found and used legal means to make the parish repair and widen no few of these, at considerable cost.

Like most such major changes the Enclosure Movement had effects good and bad. Our area certainly became a healthier place in which to live and its low-lying lands became green, pleasant and reasonably fertile. On the other hand though the fell sides lost their somewhat barren and unfriendly look, their noble lines were spoilt by no little afforestation which gave them a dull uniform look they had never had before. The late arrival of good roads and better drainage encouraged house-building on a scale which for long was too modest to be offensive, at a time when architects were far from being cranky. Economically agricultural output must have increased considerably, aided by the various agricultural improvements of the times. But the hard facts of geology and of the local climate prevented Cartmel ever becoming a flourishing area for farmers, though in the years after World War II they have become incomparably better off than in the long years before it when no few of the smaller farms lived out an existence which was pathetically precarious.

Looking back over this sketch of economic developments it becomes obvious that a variety of factors geographical and geological rendered it out of the question that in the great age of nineteenth-century industrialism Cartmel should become a great centre of money-making. Agriculture had always a limited range and a limited output and commerce never really established a significant grip on the area. Mills great and small there were, producing a wide range of products, but even the greatest of these never attained major significance. Today almost all of them are in ruins or put to other uses, the blue works at Backbarrow being the only one today which retains significant contact with an ancient past. Providentially the land of Cartmel stays unblighted by industrialism, enabling its countryside to retain the immense beauty and the natives their immense courtesy which so delighted early visitors to Lakeland.

PART II — PLACES

Allithwaite

Allithwaite derives its name from a Norse settler Eilifr, who may well have settled here in the eleventh century. His *thwaite* was probably, though not certainly, "a clearing in woodland used as meadowland" and may well have been in or near the original nucleus of the hamlet where the roads from Grange and Kents Bank today meet those from Flookburgh to Cartmel. The connection of Allithwaite with such main routes as there were, and its comparatively fertile soil give it more than usual interest for the local historian.

As we have seen Kirkhead cave is much the oldest and most interesting prehistoric site in the valley whilst close to it was the site of the early Anglian chapel which gave Kirkhead its name. In or about 1160 the abbey of Furness acquired the land on which they built the first Abbot Hall and which provided pasture for five cows, thus ensuring the brethren's milk supply. This site was invaluable for a monastery whose considerable importance and widespread possessions entailed constant journeying to and fro over the estuaries which separated Furness from the rest of Lancashire and the lands beyond, for as we have seen these crossings involved no little prospects of delay. The medieval buildings at Abbot Hall have long since disappeared, but may well have resembled those of the grange of Furness abbey much of which is still visible at Hawkshead, and which consists of a large hall with minor buildings set in an enclosure.

After the Dissolution of the monasteries Abbot Hall became for a long time a private residence, passing through various families' hands and early in this century was used as a school. There seems to be no significant remains of the medieval buildings or of the seventeenth-century residence which was built on its site, though we have interesting references to the latter in the early *Sketches of Grange*. It mentions "this once venerable building" whose "antique gables, high chimneys and mullioned windows are still regretted by those who knew it in former years. True the old oak beams and floors and spacious stair-case had suffered much from the effects of age; the rats had been allowed free warren and the grounds were over-run with brambles and nettles". There were traditions of "fair and beautiful ghosts . . . relations, they were said to be, of a certain abbot who lived in retirement here".

A new mansion was built here, partly the work of Miss Lambert, perhaps the wealthiest lady who ever lived in Cartmel, who also erected Boarbank Hall and left bequests to set up Allithwaite Church. But it was bought from her trustees by James Simpson Young who, says Stockdale, "greatly beautified both the house and grounds, and made it a handsome modern residence". This was offered for sale with very extensive adjoining properties in 1879, the catalogue for this showing how well-equipped the mansion was. There were "fifteen bedrooms including servants' rooms and dressing-rooms, the front rooms being of spacious proportions", staircases that were "massive and in accordance with the proportions of the Mansion throughout", Scullery, Cook's and Butler's pantries. Outside buildings included a Harness room and Coach House, Dog Kennels, Gun Room as well as Croquet and Tennis Lawn and Vineries "stocked with vines of choice flavour and quality". Amongst other items in the sale was Kirkhead with its "Tower or Summer House" which may have been erected by Miss Lambert. In 1915 Abbot Hall was purchased by the Methodist Guild for use as a holiday home, a function which it still fulfills.

Once the old hall had become a private residence, the need for an inn where travellers coming or going across the Sands was irrefutable and one was established across the road from the hall, at an early but unknown date. Dorothy Wordsworth, sister of the poet, was once apparently on holiday at Kents Bank, but the place was not destined to compete with Grange in this respect and subsequent buildings here were almost entirely private houses. A directory of 1876 notes "At Kents Bank are several genteel houses, fitted up for the reception of visitors. The long building once used as an hotel, is now converted into lodgings". In 1857 Kents Bank acquired a small railway station of its own.

Not far from Abbot Hall, on the other side of Humphrey Head, stands Wraysholme Tower on a low ridge which, until the enclosures of the last century, was virtually beside the sea. This is the sole major fortified medieval building in Cartmel and the only one connected with a medieval family of major social importance – the Harringtons, who acquired some little land here at the very end of the thirteenth century, though this estate seems to have been largely held by junior branches.

The family took its name from Harrington in Cumberland and established their main seat at Gleaston castle in Low Furness. For reasons which are not yet clear, John Harrington attained the rank of Peer, being summoned to Parliament from 1324 to 1345. He died in 1347 and seems to have a special affection for Cartmel priory, since instead of being buried at the priory of Conishead a few miles from the family castle, he had made for himself and his wife a most elaborate and magnificent chantry at Cartmel which was set in the equally magnificent south choir aisle which he had rebuilt (see pp. 35-7). His immediate heirs were also peers but the male line ended with Lord William Harrington who died in 1457, leaving only a daughter whose marriage took the family estates to the Marquess of Dorset.

These grandees were much involved in major affairs far distant from Lonsdale North of the Sands. At the battle of Agincourt Lord William Harrington was present accompanied by ten men-at-arms, as were other members of his family with similar contingents, which may well have included some Cartmel men. Sir William's will is the earliest one from our area to have survived; it includes major benefactions to the family priory of Conishead and a useful gift to Cartmel priory then in financial difficulties (see p. 20). However it is unlikely that these great men spent much time at Wraysholme for when they were in Lancashire their seat would be their much more spacious castle of Gleaston, though in their journeys across the Sands,

Plate 9 (a and b) — Stained Glass in Bowness Church.

a. Sir William Thornburgh and his wife.

b. The Prior of Cartmel.

c. Lindale and Castlehead before the coming of the Railway.

Plate 10b — John Wilkinson, iron master (by L. F. Abbott). *(National Portrait Gallery)*

Plate 10a — Christopher Rawlinson, scholar, died 1733. He added the great door to Cark Hall, and the summer house.

Plate 11 — Vanished Chapels.

a. Lindale.

b. Field Broughton.

c. Flookburgh, demolished 1776-7.

d. Flookburgh Chapel 1777-1900.

Plate 12a — Wraysholme Tower, a late 15th Century pele tower.

Plate 12b — Cark Hall, a late Elizabethan mansion, with its summer house.

doubtless Wraysholme was often found useful for brief residence. Though the Harringtons were no longer here to join them, we know that Cartmel men fought at the famous field of Flodden, for a curious Tudor ballad about it tells of English warriors

> From Silverdale and Kent Sand side
> Where soil is sold with cockle shells
> For Cartmel eke and Conneyside (Conishead)
> And fellows fierce from Furneys fells.

This ballad tells us that the men from "Lancashire for the most part" were led by "the lusty Stanley", a reference to Thomas Stanley, second Earl of Derby, whose father's support of the new King Henry VII had led him to acquire no little property in Lancashire, including Wraysholme tower. However it is doubtful if the Stanleys used the place themselves, and certain that fairly early in the sixteenth century it was leased to one Hugh Dicconson, whose family hailed from the Leyland area, and was bought by a descendant of his late in the reign of Elizabeth. It is very likely that the two lay-brothers of this name at Cartmel priory, who escaped the grim fate of most of their brethren in 1536 (see pp. 23-4) were members of this family, which was certainly much suspected of conservative religious views (in 1539 a Dicconson of Cartmel was arrested and sent up to London). However, as is usual with the "church-papists" of these days, outwardly at least the family conformed with Anglican worship. In 1568 we find one Hugh Dicconson of Wraysholme claiming of right a pew in Cartmel church. The last of the family known to be linked with Wraysholme was one Francis Dickinson who was baptised at Cartmel church in 1635 and buried in there in 1714. After this time, as happened no little in our area, a place which had been for long a residence for gentry degenerated into a mere farmhouse.

Wraysholme Tower today (Pl. 12a) is very little damaged by time and has very recently been given a useful restoration. It is all of late fifteenth century date with the possible exception of a small door which may be a hundred years or so earlier, and it follows a plan of which northern England can show many similar examples. It is oblong (measuring 40 feet by 28 feet) with a projecting garderobe and has three storeys. The ground floor, entered by a very narrow door has walls 4 feet thick and was used to store cattle and other valuables in time of war. A stair in the wall leads to the floor above which was the main living room above which is the top floor from which there is access to the roof with its prominent turret used primarily as a beacon.[13] It is very probable that the tower at Wraysholme, in its present form like the very similar ones at Hazelslack and Arnside, was constructed after the immense scare caused by the landing at Piel of the great invasion force of Lambert Simnel in 1487. The predecesor of the present building was probably not a fortified one but a

---

[13] For very long indeed the Lake Counties were never free from the danger of ferocious Scots raids, so there developed an elaborate warning system of beacons to give notice of the raiders' approach, key sites here being Piel Castle, so prominent on our horizon, and one at the southern tip of Hampsfell near the clubhouse of the modern golf club.

simple hall which may have been on the site of the present farm-house. Until about a century ago in a window of the latter were three small quarries of late sixteenth-century stained glass depicting the initials HD for Hugh Dicconson, and the eagle and child and the eagle's claw which were the badge and crest of the Stanley family (Fig. 4). Since Stockdale's day these have disappeared (some thirty years ago they were said to be in a house in Ambleside); news of their present home would be very welcome.

FIG. 4   Glass formerly at Wraysholme Tower.

There is no reason to think that Wraysholme Tower ever heard the sound of gunfire except on one occasion. An interesting and probably reliable tradition avers that it was attacked by the Roundheads, a body of whom are known to have passed this way en route to Furness from Thurland late in 1643. It is most interesting that another tradition maintains that Roundhead forces spent a night in camp in two fields below Boarbank very near Wraysholme and adjoining the main road into Furness, which, to this day, are called Oliver field and Cromwell field. These forces were in a very great hurry to attack their enemies in Furness and return as speedily as possible to the siege of Thurland, so they would certainly not have besieged Wraysholme, but may well have fired at it, since its owners at this time was the conservative Dicconson family who were unlikely to have had an affection for the Roundhead cause.

Of other residences in the Allithwaite area the most substantial is Boarbank Hall. Until just over a century ago there was here only a farm-house which had for long housed members of the old and rather prolific family called Barrow, one of whose early members is pictured with other canons of Cartmel priory in a panel of stained glass in the east window of Bowness Parish church (see p. 88). After the middle of the seventeenth century the property passed through a number of different hands. In 1837 there came to live here the immensely wealthy Miss Mary Winfield Lambert. She died exactly twenty years later and the property was sold to one Henry Chandler who rebuilt the front of the house after its destruction by fire and added an extensive north wing. After two other owners had held it – John Ratcliffe, M.P. and Joseph Bliss, M.P. – in 1921 nuns of the Order of Our Lady of Lourdes, following the Rule of St Augustine which had been observed at Cartmel priory in its monastic days, purchased the place. Their programme combined an elaborate round of liturgical worship with care for convalescents, to which was added the reception of guests in need of rest. In 1955, several of the sisters having qualified as nurses, a new phase opened with extension of the community's work to the care of the sick, mostly from the surrounding area, who were housed in an extension to the existing building. Their devotion and invaluable service to society has won for the community a very deep and wide affection.

Not far from Boarbank is Birkby, the name of which, as we have seen (see p. 3), denotes a very ancient settlement and which may be a place mentioned in *Domesday Book*. Its history is very obscure indeed throughout medieval times. Later the hall there belonged to the Fletchers, a fairly important yeoman family, and may well have been built or re-built in the latter half of the seventeenth century like so many others, but ancient disrepair and extensive modernization have left little remains of its antiquity; an old plaster ceiling was destroyed (perhaps having become irrepairably decayed) about the end of the last century. The iron gates and their gate-posts at the entrance to the Hall originally belonged to the churchyard of the church at Flookburgh, and were moved here about sixty years ago. Fields below the hall may be worthy of archaeological examination.

A local tradition, the authenticity of which it is quite impossible to check, avers that the last wolf in England was killed in the Allithwaite area. Given the fact that such animals became extinct here in times when no records of such things were kept, and when local conditions made it virtually impossible to tell which, in fact, was the last animal of its kind to depart this life in England, it is clearly impossible to give total credence to the tradition. But informed scientific opinion would accept the fact that our area was one very suitable for wolves' habitat, and the very scanty local population and wild countryside makes it likely enough that wolves continued to exist here long after they were extinct in no few more populous regions. If as is likely, the tradition held that the killer of the wolf was one of the Harringtons of Wraysholme, this is likely enough, as the skill, arms and armour possessed by such nobles at this time would be highly desirable if not absolutely essential to accomplish such a feat.[14]

However even if we are prepared to accept the tradition in skeleton form it is important not to swallow the mass of local detail with which it has been encrusted by the Victorian authoress of the long poem termed "The Last Wolf", most of which cannot be taken seriously as factual, albeit providing a fine example of the donation of verisimilitude "to an otherwise bald and unconvincing narrative".

In this poetical effusion prominence is given to the very noble cliff named Humphrey Head, on whose great beauty no few have commented. Until quite

[14] Boarbank is said to owe its name to the fact that it was here that the wolf was despatched. This is neither provable nor impossible; Ekwall produces no explanation of the meaning of this place-name.

recently it attracted some little attention for no little time through the presence on its western side of a spring whose waters were long utilised by the sick. It came to be termed the Holy Well, but there is no reason to believe that it was used in medieval times; an early reference to it in the fascinating Household Account Book of Swarthmoor in 1674 terms it "Cartmel well". In 1700 a writer mentions it as "a spring of purging waters in a village called Rougham near the sands where a crossing is made into Furness". In 1750 Bp. Richard Pococke records rather oddly "I set out (from Lancaster) in the afternoon and we went three miles to the Strand over which we crossed into Fourness to Cartlone (*sic*) near Cartmell where there is a mineral spring and a great Latin school". It is clear from the early guide-books of the last century that major interest in the spring was shown by the lead miners from Alston on the far Cumbrian border for whose ailments it was apparently beneficial. A Victorian writer notes "the spring issues from a fissure in the rock within a few feet of the base of the rock and has long been celebrated for its curative properties in gout, bilious and cutaneous complaints". Probably at some time in the last century a small house was erected near the well, but fifty years ago this was in ruinous condition and has since been demolished. Before the outbreak of the Second World War for a while water from the well was sent in milk churns to Morecambe where it was put on sale, apparently not without success. At the present time it has been for some time totally neglected. A Victorian report in the *Chemical Journal* noted the specific gravity of the water as 1005·83, with 508·5199 grains to the gallon, the principal ingredients being chloride sodium $41\frac{1}{2}$, sulphate of lime 11, chloride of magnesium $5\frac{1}{2}$. It was noted that of the foreign spas that of Wiesbaden had waters of similar composition.

Right down to very modern times the population of Allithwaite was quite minute and far from rich, so it is not surprising that it had to wait for a wealthy Victorian to provide it with its own church. This was Miss Mary Winfield Lambert whose elaborate will of 1851 made complex arrangements for the erection of "a Church or chapel" with a dwelling for "the Minister" and a School house "to be used solely for the education of the children of the labouring classes of the Township of Lower Allithwaite and "a residence for the Mistress". The nomination of "the Curate or Minister" was to be vested "in the Bishop of Chester and no other person" (Chester was the diocese in which Cartmel was at this time situate). The church of St Mary, Templand was built in 1865 and its district assigned in the following year.

Broughton and Newton

Broughton

Broughton is very easily the commonest of our place-names and is of English not Scandinavian origin. It has several allied meanings, but here probably means "the estate or farmstead by the stream". Given the considerable lack of streams to that upper part of the valley to which Broughton pertains, the fact that Hampsfield Hall was certainly one of the two oldest estates in the valley (going back to pre-Conquest times) and that here is a largish pond and remarkably active beck (the only one on this side of the valley), the present writer has little doubt that the site of the original "farmstead by the stream" was that now occupied by Hampstead Hall.[15]

The estate for long passed through varied ownership, but ultimately to the Thornburghs who held it from the early fifteenth century for over two hundred years. They took their name from their place of origin in Yorkshire, but a branch of the family later established itself in south Westmorland. Amongst the panels of glass in the great east window of Bowness parish church is an attractive one of a knight and his lady, obligingly inscribed "William Thornboro and his Wyff", showing both of them displaying their family coat of arms (Pl. 9a). Since that of the lady belongs to the Broughton family, we can safely conclude that the William Thornburgh here depicted is the one who is known to have married Elizabeth Broughton, and died in 1523, and whose main lands were in the Kendal area. After the dissolution of the monasteries the Thornburghs acquired some ex-monastic property but conservative in their religion as the little memorial to Etheldred Thornburgh still visible in Cartmel priory shows (see p. 39). In 1636 the then owner, yet another William Thornburgh, sold Hampsfield Hall.

As so often happened in our area this attractive mansion fell on evil days in the eighteenth and early nineteenth century. Today it retains no little of its picturesque external appearance but has largely lost its antique fittings. It is highly likely that this seventeenth-century house was built on a fresh site a little to the north of a medieval one. The invaluable Stockdale tells us that about 1814, during the absence of the owner the tenant of Hampsfield Hall pulled down the nearby medieval tower. It is quite possible that this early abode was not a simple pele tower, but may well have formed part of a larger complex such as that which we can still see at Beetham Hall; excavation here might well prove to be interesting, though no very spectacular finds are likely.

On the fell above Hampsfield Hall and some way south of it is the Hospice, a little square tower with stairs leading to a flat roof from which a magnificent panorama is visible. It was built by the Rev Thomas Remington vicar of Cartmel from 1835 to 1854, a former Fellow of Trinity College Cambridge. He had taken a great delight in the view from the top of Hampsfell to which he climbed with great frequency; he cut out cardboard letters to enable the local mason to carve the Greek inscription over the hospice door.

Just to the north of Hampsfield Hall an old road from Lindale runs westward towards Wood Broughton intersecting the equally ancient route from Cartmel to Newton. The area here is known as St Andrew Moor, possibly because there was originally here a chantry chapel dedicated to this saint; (such things were quite often situate at crossroads). Nearby is a large boulder called Egg Pudding Stone, which has obscure folklore behind it: some say that tradition avers that it turns round when the priory clock strikes midnight, cynics say that it only does this when it hears the clock strike! Very recently the boulder has been shifted from its original position in the interests of road-widening.

[15] Hampsfield and Hampsfell contain the name of the Norseman called Hamr.

Undoubtedly the oldest of the fairly numerous mansions in the Broughton area is Broughton Hall, which for several centuries was evidently the residence of the Knipes; though it is likely enough that some parts of the present building are very old, others have been destroyed or modernized, so that its architectural history is very uncertain. Of the rest the most spectacular is Broughton Lodge which was built about 1780-90, apparently for the first directors of the Backbarrow cotton mill, who presumably laid out the grounds. Broughton Grange has a date stone of 1737 but has been greatly reconstructed and Broughton House is apparently mid-eighteenth century. Grey Rigg (whither was transported from Cark Hall a stone carved with the arms of Curwen Rawlinson (d. 1689) and his wife) has much nineteenth century work, as has Broughton Bank (largely the work of Sir John Hibbert in 1880-2).

This poorish and very thinly populated area understandably waited long for its own place of worship. In his will dated 14 June 1731 Miles Brown left £50 for erecting a chapel in Broughton, an act which ultimately led to the erection of a very simple edifice (Pl. 11b) that was dedicated on 30 June 1745, extended somewhat about a century later and made a separate parish in 1875, after having had its own burial ground since 1818. In *The Rural Deanery of Cartmel* (1892) it is noted that "a handsome new church in place of the present building which is rapidly falling into decay, is about to be built". This was the gift of Mrs T. J. Hibbert and is a fine example of Austin and Paley work, with attendant woodwork and embroidery which has attracted much praise from the experts.

Near the church on some waste ground on the opposite side of the round is a circular stone structure recently restored. Such things – known as "pounds" – were used to temporarily house farm animals which had strayed from their rightful residences and were quite common in our area before the enclosures of the late eighteenth and early nineteenth centuries led to the destruction of the hitherto very extensive areas of unfenced land (another pound, in somewhat dilapidated condition can be seen at Rosthwaite, a few hundred yards below Cark Hall).

Newton

As we have seen Newton has the distinction of being one of the minute number of places in Cartmel mentioned in *Domesday Book* and its name denotes a settlement of Anglian origin. It owes its existence very largely to the fact that it is situated at the junction of the road which traverses Cartmel from south to north, with what must have been a very ancient if not very popular track which comes from the Winster valley up the fell-side to go on to the Newby Bridge area. However, Newton is situated in what is certainly the most infertile part of Cartmel, with little but fell and moorland at hand, so it is not surprising that the place never had more than a very small number of inhabitants and no notable halls or mansions. The inn here was probably built soon after the increase in traffic to the area that followed the creation of the great turnpike from Lindale in 1818-20. In and about the eighteenth century weaving was established here in some cottages apparently built for the purpose. A number of tracks, some of them old pack-horse tracks, can still be traced leading towards Bigland and thence down to a major crossing of the Leven, several houses in the area show evident signs of being connected with this traffic. High Cark Hall has an attractive facade of early eighteenth century date, replete with stone mullioned windows, and inside a massive ingle-nook little altered. The river Ay rises just north of the hamlet in very unobtrusive fashion, going underground for a time to emerge not far from High Cark.

Staveley – Not far from Newton is Staveley-in-Cartmel, a miniscule place. Even today much of the area is quite heavily wooded and very little cultivated. A rental of 1509 shows that Cartmel priory owned most of the land here and had a number of tenants who were very far indeed from being substantial. The little church is charmingly hidden amongst trees and originated as a small chapel at an unknown date, perhaps in the early seventeenth century – the first known reference to it is in 1618 when one Henry Longmire was "reader". It seems to have long lacked any adequate endowment, a deficiency partially remedied by having a priest-schoolmaster with a school at the chapel and an ancient custom whereby the principal inhabitants of the parish took turns in providing him with board and lodging. The architectural history of the chapel is obscure though it is known to have been restored in 1678 and 1693. The present building has very few signs of antiquity but is not unattractive.

Bigland means "the barley land" and, like nearby Haverthwaite ("the oats *thwaite*"), reminds us that here we have soil where corn does not flourish. There is no village or hamlet but a hall perched high up on the hills, held since Tudor times by a family which took their surname from the place. In Wilson Bradyll Bigland they produced the only admiral bred in Cartmel, some of whose interesting belongings are still preserved. The original building was probably a small hall of Tudor date of which the walls remain along with a large fireplace and a massive beam which is carved with the initials I (for J) B and MB and a date in Arabic numerals which is a considerable problem, some optimists believing it to be 1166. But the second figure is by no means certainly a 1, and it is quite impossible that the house is as old as this, whilst, even if it was, at this time in England the numerals in use were Roman not Arabic. In the early eighteenth century marriage to an heiress enabled the owner to erect a fine new wing. Perhaps, though not certainly, at this time one part of the Hall came to be used as a court room, being provided with two nearby lock-up cells, which have recently been demolished.

Cark and Holker

Cark

According to *English Place-Name Elements* the name of Cark derives from the Celtic word *carrec*, meaning a rock. This accords perfectly with the traditional pronunciation of the word, but is not convincing, firstly because the geographical situation of place is at the foot of low hills with no obvious rock around, and secondly because the name is also found as that of a hamlet just north of Cartmel village which is traditionally called High or Over Cark, to distinguish it from the village of Cark which until comparatively recently was sometimes termed Nether Cark or Low Cark. Accordingly it has been suggested that the name may derive from a lost name of the beck now called the Ay, which becomes sizeable near High Cark and is a prominent feature of Cark-in-Cartmel where it is called Cark Beck and widens out into a small creek that runs in the Leven estuary. Here, as we have seen, the lay-out was complicated when, almost certainly about the end of Elizabeth's reign the owner of Cark Hall made a channel from the Ay that ran from several hundred yards north of the Hall past it to high ground on the east side of the village where it worked a paper mill before making its way to the sea. In Stockdale's day there were in the village "no fewer than twelve bridges over the river and the races in addition to the two bridges at Carke Hall and five constructed by the railway company – nineteen in all".

There is no doubt that Cark was virtually non-existent when the noble mansion known as Cark Hall (Pl. 12b) was founded, though there may have been a few small houses on the elevated ground near the present inn. It seems certain that the original hall was built by one Thomas Pickering (he was married at Cartmel in 1571) and probably belonged to the old south Westmorland family of this name. Though the point is not one which can be proved with certainty in the present writer's opinion, he was a "church-papist" (i.e. a Roman Catholic paying nominal allegiance to the Established Church) who settled in this very lonely and isolated spot, for strategic religious reasons of which the chief was the ready and undisturbed access to the sea provided here by the creek known as Cark Beck.

Thomas Pickering's daughter Anne in 1602 married Robert Curwen of Myreside Hall below Flookburgh. Her husband belonged to a junior branch of the great Cumbrian family and moved to Cark Hall after his father-in-law's death. Robert left a very long will (1649) which Stockdale prints, and was succeeded by his very well-to-do nephew Robert Rawlinson, a barrister of Gray's Inn (d. 1665). The next owner was his eldest son Curwen Rawlinson (1641-89) whose wife Anne was a niece of the famous General Monk, being the daughter of his brother Nicholas Monk, Bishop of Hereford. The elaborate inscription on her family memorial in Cartmel priory church tells us that Anne showed "divine patience under the tortures of the stone" and "resigned her heavenly soul" on 27 Sept. 1691. Four years later her son Monk followed her to burial there and the family possessions passed to a Christopher Rawlinson (1677-1733) an attractive and interesting man (Pl. 10a), eminent enough to secure a place in the *Dictionary of National Biography*. He was an early student of Anglo-Saxon and whilst in residence at Cark Hall worked vigorously on collecting material for the history of Westmorland and North Lancashire which has been largely lost. Disappointingly he left instructions that he was to be buried in St Alban's abbey. Most unfortunately since he was unmarried and left no will, his property passed to five cousins none of whom took over Cark Hall, which steadily deteriorated into being a mere farm house, losing no little of its past glories, though there yet remains the noble main door with the coat of arms of Christopher Rawlinson quartering those of Curwen and Monk, with the Rawlinson crest – a shelldrake proper, in its beak an escallop argent. At Grey Rigg there is to be seen another coat of arms with the arms of Curwen Rawlinson impaled with those of his wife which were removed there in the last century from their rightful position over another door at Cark Hall. A recently discovered document which it is very difficult to dismiss as fiction shows us that there appeared at Cark in Christopher Rawlinson's time a highly mysterious French aristocrat who refused to reveal his name even on his deathbed and who was regularly visited by an English peer, who treated him with enormous deference, not sitting down in his presence and always speaking to him bare-headed (see App. III). Who this stranger was is one of the most intriguing mysteries in the history of Cartmel.

The Hall is easily the most picturesque of all the ancient residences, having not only multitudinous mullioned windows but a truly magnificent entrance put in by Christopher Rawlinson with Ionic columns supporting a large arch in which is set his large coat of arms and crest. It stands on a noble set of steps on which are now two rectangular stones. On the western side is a bulky wing added to the place probably in the seventeenth century. The Hall has sadly lost almost all its ancient furnishings, the one great exception being the very fine panelled front bedroom. In the room beneath was for a long time a mighty oak refectory table of late seventeenth century date brought here in post-Rawlinson times which quite recently has been moved to Holker Hall. A fine but somewhat damaged mahogany corner cupboard with most elegant shelves and a semi-circular head painted with a vigorous picture of Neptune and his horses which was discovered in a Cark outhouse and rescued by the writer's father, almost certainly came from Cark Hall.

Behind the Hall are remains of a fairly large garden stretching up the hillside, part of which is terraced. At its top corner is a small, picturesque, square building of two storeys (Pl. 12b) with large rectangular windows and a door which has a stone shield that bears a monogram similar to that on one of the ancient prints of Christopher Rawlinson (Pl. 10a). It may well have been part summer house part library and commands truly magnificent views; it has long been roofless.

On the western side of the Hall were, until recently, two very interesting outbuildings of seventeenth century date, in excellent repair, whose demolition the local "powers-that-be" allowed in one of their rarish lapses of judgement. The larger of these adjoined the road with foundations on huge boulders. Its ground floor was a shippon and was entered by a door which adjoined the entrance to the drive of the house. The upper floor which had stone mullioned windows rather more elaborate than those below was probably the sleeping place of the labourers and was entered by a simple external stone stair at its western end. Some thirty yards further west aligned against the boundary wall of the farm was a smaller building of one storey with a few stone-mullioned windows that was probably used for storage of farm implements. The opposite side of the road is lined by a range of modern buildings, but behind them is an unobtrusive but fine barn with a cruck roof which is probably part of the original construction i.e. of late sixteenth century date. Very recently it has been converted into a dwelling. The area below the two streams that run in front of the hall is known as Rosthwaite and has the remains of a pound.

There was no sign of any growth in the small population of Cark for very long, though in the seventeenth century a few rather minor houses were built, including a small one later built into Cark House. The latter is a large Georgian building which has a fine façade and was almost certainly built by James Stockdale's namesake and grandfather. On the little hilltop behind it within the writer's memory existed remains of a polygonal summerhouse of classical design surrounded by a border of periwinkles and a hedge.

As we have seen (see pp. 56-8) a most unexpected development in the history of the village occurred in the early seventeenth century when a paper mill was built here, whilst at the end of the eighteenth century came greater change it was decided to erect lower down the village a mighty cotton mill with a considerable number of attendant cottages. Of the three rows of the latter built along the steep slope north west of the site of the mill the top and bottom ones – known as High Row and Low Row – survive and continue to serve their original purpose, but Middle Row was largely demolished, though one of its walls is used as a boundary to what is now a garden. The mill itself was largely destroyed by fire in 1936. Its remains, along with the cottages on either side of the yard in front of it and the picturesque little gatehouse through which the yard was entered were later demolished in the interests of modern housing.

Holker

The name Holker is said to mean "the hollow marsh" which sounds likely enough, for most of the area consists of very low-lying land situate between hills beside the Leven estuary on one side and the line of fell country dominated by Howbarrow on the other, which even today is very scantily provided with houses apart from Holker Hall and its satellite buildings So marshy was the ground and for long so unimportant was Cark that until recent times no good road ran to connect the latter with the Backbarrow area, whilst even today Holker has no shop. As we have noted (see p. 8), it is quite possible that this place is mentioned in *Domesday Book* in conjunction with Birkby, but this does not necessarily imply the existence of a village or hamlet. At first the only building of any size in this area was the grange established at an unknown date by Cartmel priory that came to be know as Frith Hall. It stands on the shore of the estuary near an old route which led across the latter into Furness, and would have had a barn or barns, a jetty and some domestic accommodation to which the fragmentary remains visible there today doubtless pertain.

The one major development in the history of Holker, and it was of great local significance, was the establishment on its present site of Holker Hall, an initiative taken by Cartmel priory's well-to-do and pious benefactor George Preston at an unknown date in the early seventeenth century (he bought various properties in this area in 1610). The elder branch of his family had earlier acquired the site of Furness abbey (establishing itself in a great mansion there) along with very considerable local properties which included the port of Piel, from which they seem to have maintained links with the Continent as the monks had done before them. But about 1680, these Furness properties were confiscated, for the picturesque reason that their owner had sought to convey them to the Jesuits and passed to the Holker branch of the family, thus making the owners of Holker Hall incomparably the wealthiest family in North Lancashire, a position they have since maintained with ease.

The Preston family hailed from Preston Patrick not far over the Westmorland area, and one Christopher Preston (d. 1594) acquired some of the property in Cartmel formerly belonging to the priory about 1556. His grandson, George Preston, as we have seen was at first a "church papist" and finally an avowed Roman Catholic. He died in 1640 and was succeeded by his son Thomas (d. 1678), described as "always a constant Protestant" who suffered much for his loyalty to King Charles. His elder son George died soon after his succession to the estates, which now passed to the younger son, Thomas, and were swollen by acquisition of the confiscated Furness lands. He had no sons but a daughter, Elizabeth, who brought new owners to Holker by marrying Sir William Lowther of Marske in North Yorkshire, a member of a junior branch of the great Lakeland family. Of him little is known.

His only child, Sir Thomas (d. 1745) moved up the social scale somewhat by marrying one Elizabeth, a daughter of the Duke of Devonshire. He and his wife seem to have been colourful people. In a vivid study of Holker Hall in the *Lonsdale Magazine* for 1820, the writer regrets lack of biographical material about Sir Thomas but notes "the wonderful tales of his necromantic feats which tradition has preserved are evident proof that his attainments were superior to those of his neighbours ... instead of obtaining an account of his learning and his knowledge, we find nothing but tales of his conjuring tricks .... In short what Bacon was to the kingdom in general in the sixteenth century, Sir Thomas was to Cartmel in the eighteenth". His pursuits also included horse-racing (did Cartmel races originate in his time?). His wife – known as Lady Betty Lowther – had a passion for very long walks not shared by the footmen who shared the duty of escorting, at least one of whom expired through his exertions on this duty. Sir Thomas's successor was his short-lived son Sir William of whom an attractive bust is preserved in the Town Choir of the Priory church; its attendant inscription notes that he was "the last of his family in the male line, who, however respectable soever for the antiquity of it, was more so for the excellancy of his virtue".

From him the estates now passed to his cousins, Lord George and Lord Frederick Cavendish, neither of whom left any issue, and then to Lord George Augustus Henry Cavendish who became Earl of Burlington in 1831, but died three years later. In this title and in the possession of the Holker estates he was followed by Sir William Cavendish (1808-91) who went on to become 7th Duke of Devonshire (1858-91). Holker was now very high up the social tree and "the old Duke", as locals called him in the writer's boyhood, was still remembered with great affection. Vigorous, competent and kindly he developed the rich family resources with the aid of the new-fangled railways, interested himself in politics and in the growing university life. He was made K.G. in 1858 and P.C. in 1876. In his time Holker Hall saw immense social activity and a coming and going of great figures unparalleled in Cartmel history, including the great Mr Gladstone whose curious pastime of cutting down trees was indulged in Holker woods. Some invaluable glimpses of life at Holker Hall at this time are contained in the published selections from the voluminous diaries of Lady Frederick Cavendish, a singularly sensitive and attractive person whose brutally murdered husband is commemorated in a noble memorial in Cartmel Priory church. High up on a slope below Howbarrow, whence can be seen a stupendous panorama of great nobility the "old Duke" had constructed for himself a simple timber seat that came to be known as "the Duke's seat", which has recently disintegrated. For some time now Holker Hall and its estates have been held by a junior line of the family, the present owner being Mr Hugh Cavendish.

Holker Hall has a far more complex architectural history than any of the other major houses of our area, largely because its owners had so much more money and were much more interested in keeping up with current fashion. It is likely enough that the original house was a fairly simple one with the multitudinous stone mullioned windows of which we have so many examples, but of it there are no recognizable remains, though we can still see in the house a few magnificently carved twisted columns of seventeenth century date. Much of the Hall was apparently rebuilt in the early eighteenth century when a north wing was added and formal gardens laid out which were in the taste of the time. These were adorned with what the *Lonsdale Magazine* of 1820 terms "a quantity of excellent specimens of statues" which "have recently been removed in compliment to the chaster and more rational taste of modern improvements". But Lord George Augustus Cavendish (1783-93) added "an elegant modern Gothic wing" and replaced the formal gardens by "natural" ones. About 1815 came more alterations which included facing the front of the house with Roman cement, shown in the aquatint of the *Lonsdale Magazine* of 1820 (Pl. 13b) which adds the comment "this building, however, is copied from no style that ever prevailed in any period of English history". In 1840 Lord Burlington employed the Kendal architect Thomas Webster to alter and reface the hall in what was a rather Tudor style. Unhappily during the night of 10 March 1871 a most ferocious fire broke out which destroyed the west wing of the house, and much of its contents, including an appalling number of works of art including some pictures of high value and portraits of considerable historic interest. However money and enthusiasm for immediate rebuilding were both there in abundance and the much damaged house was quickly restored from designs by the north country architects Austin and Paley "their outstanding work, red sandstone in the Elizabethan style" comments Pevsner.

The gardens of Holker Hall are of special interest thanks to friendly soil and climate and the considerable interest in them shown by no few of their past owners, notably Lord George Cavendish who was a keen collector of horticultural rarities. In Victorian times the number of gardeners employed was quite large enough to furnish a cricket team that was on occasion taken over to play their opposite numbers at Chatsworth. Large, indeed too large, if local tradition be correct, were some gigantic pots ordered for the Hall by a certain head gardener who unfortunately gave the measurement of the circumference as being that of the diameter! For some years now the Hall and gardens have been open to the public. If the former has no architecture of any great antiquity, it is still well supplied with attractive furniture and china and has no few pictures.

Relations between the Hall and the villagers around it in Victorian times were run on conventional lines, being patriarchial but cordial. Just as then at Haverthwaite any local schoolboys who did not doff their caps to members of "the gentry" whom they met in the street were likely to be punished by their schoolmaster, so young girls who did not stop to curtsey when the Duchess' carriage went past in Cark might be in trouble at school soon thereafter. On the other hand the school at Holker, the Institute at Cark, (till World War II so much used), as well as the magnificent new church at Flookburgh, were all gifts of the Cavendishes. At the Hall was kept a curious hearse-shaped fire-engine towed by a horse and manned by the locals. Of it, Nash's invaluable Almanac notes "The Brigade is a voluntary one and finds its own uniform and appliances, towards which, and an annual supper, they are very glad of any subscriptions the public may think them deserving of". The public was also informed that "Harness is kept at the engine house, Holker, for the purpose, but horses should be sent". The details of local organizations in the land of Cartmel at this time given in the almanac make fascinating reading, being very numerous and varying widely in scope. Thus we find a Committee for Lighting the Town of Cartmel, the Cartmel Marquee Company, various schools and sports clubs, nearly two dozen "Literary and Philanthropic Societies" and a score or so Sick Clubs and Benefit Societies including the Ancient Order of Foresters (Court Evergreen), as well as a quite ancient Cartmel Savings Group which issued noble certificates (Pl. 15a). Almost all these, like the Holker Charity School (App. V) are now extinct.

Cartmel (Churchtown)

As we have already seen the word "Cartmel" has denoted different things at different times. At first it was a "land" – merely a strip of territory, and then for a while a "barony" i.e. a feudal unit. With the foundation of the priory ambiguity developed, as Cartmel might mean the area of land held here by the monastery or the place in which the latter was situate. But it is important to note that in the interest of clarity the latter came to be termed "Churchtown", following herein deep-rooted local custom which used the Scandinavian equivalent for this purpose ("Kirkby") to indicate a place with a major church. Thus the early parish registers of Cartmel not infrequently use the form "Churchtown" to indicate a place of residence and in 1696 the Lancashire Association Oath Rolls uses "Kirkby in Cartmell" as a main heading, with Templand and "Church Town" beneath. However in process of time this usage has fallen into disuse as has the similar ancient one which formerly termed Kendal "Kirkby Kendal".

If the present village of Cartmel has become so celebrated for its beauty and placidity this is principally because its remote situation and lack of any industrial potential has left it down to modern times largely unspoilt either by expansion or rebuilding, whilst very recently the local authorities have mostly, if not wholly, been very aware of this importance of holding the vandals at bay. Should one of the canons of the priory return to the village today, he might well be surprised at the continued smallness of the place. The majestic church itself is almost unaltered as is the gatehouse and though the cloister buildings have gone, no few minor ones of monastic days still exist in part behind modern roughcast. The line of most of the old monastic boundary can be traced, though very little indeed of the original wall is now visible (Fig. 5).

Of post-Reformation structures the most curious and unusual is the lock-up some thirty yards up the road that runs north from the Post Office. It is some fifteen feet high lit only by a very small window very high up. Almost certainly its use was very largely for the drunk. To this day grosser crimes, notably of violence are very rare in the area (only very recently indeed have villagers found it essential to lock their front doors when they go out) but in ancient times the position of Cartmel made it an ideal centre for locals to meet each other and quaff alcoholic liquor, and led to an abundance of places where alcohol was to be had.

Although the tiny number of streets which the village, along with its majestic church and little square and the gently flowing river Ay provide a galaxy of picturesque views, the buildings themselves are mostly unpretentious apart from the monastic gate-house (see p. 40). Outside the latter, in the usual medieval manner, was a piece of open ground with a cross on steps, round which on due occasion clustered market stalls. The original medieval cross shaft here was destroyed (probably by the Roundheads). The history of the market at Cartmel is of no great significance. There is no doubt that the very scanty population of the place and the fact that the only road of any significance for outside traffic, was that which ran by Flookburgh, meant that the latter was much the more suitable place for a market-place. It is not certain that the market which, it was stated in 1292, that William Marshall acquired for Cartmel, was held at Churchtown. Although Sir William Lowther acquired a charter to this end in 1730-1, his venture seems not to have been successful and its resumption in 1820 was also not permanent.

Few of the houses call for special mention. If at the Dissolution some rich man had acquired the prior's house (Priory Close) as quite often happened elsewhere, we might well have it still intact. But no-one seems to have wanted it until the late seventeenth century, by which time the original roof and its timbers had gone. But at this time, someone not short of money (possibly one of the Biglands) re-furbished it, providing *inter alia* a magnificent oak staircase still intact and a large corner cupboard. A Georgian owner imposed the present façade on the house which, like its neighbours on either side, retains much walling likely to date from monastic times. The house on the north probably provided accommodation for horses on the ground floor and travellers above it, and contains a small door of medieval date. Most of the lesser houses, notably those in the square, are of uncertain date; those around its

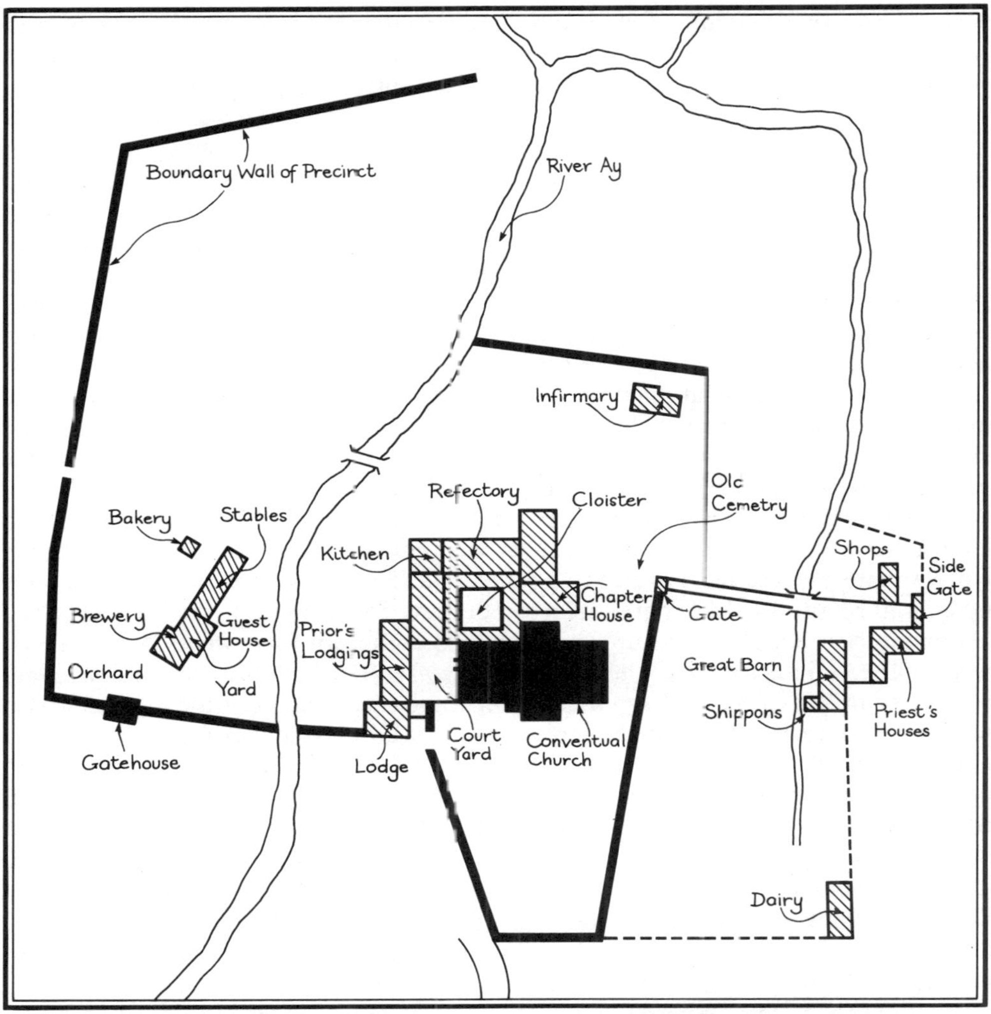

CARTMEL (CHURCHTOWN)

FIG. 5. Conjectural diagram of the layout of the Priory of Cartmel.

Known structure   Conjectural structure

Owing to the total absence of known historical and archaeological evidence on the history, position and form of almost all the monastic buildings, it is inevitable that the diagram given above has had to rely very heavily on conjecture, so it must not be taken as giving anything more then a very general and tentative picture of its subject. It is hoped to publish shortly as detailed a discussion of the subject as known material allows.

north-west corner belong largely if not wholly to the late seventeenth century, and include one with a good door and date-stone of 1658. Perhaps somewhere near here was formerly a little medieval chapel, mentioned just before the Dissolution.

On the south side of the town at the corner of Causeway End and the Cark Road is what was originally a barn, which has very recently been converted into two houses. It was probably that used for theatrical performances of which, in the eighteenth and nineteenth centuries at least, Cartmel was not bereft; tradition claims that Mrs Siddons once performed there. At the end of the Causeway opposite the barn may be seen an attractive square stone announcing that the distance to Lancaster over Sands is 15 miles and to Ulverston over Sands is 7 miles; it may well be of the same age as the similar one at Headless Cross which is dated 1836. The not unattractive institute near the Church was opened in 1865.

It is very likely that at Cartmel, a small very informal school was kept in the monastic church before the dissolution of the priory as it was after it, when the churchwardens and sidesmen ran it, appointing and paying the master, pupils mostly being taught free of charge for long. However there is no doubt that the demand for its services was mostly very limited, the local population being small and almost totally devoted to agriculture wherein literacy was no great asset. Unfortunately the school with fewish scholars and minor endowments, never built up a great reputation like that at nearby Hawkshead. In 1624, as we have seen, the Gatehouse was bought for its use and remained such until 1790 when a school room was built. As late as 1914 the *Victoria County History* notes that its scholars comprised only 15 boys and 13 girls. By this time there had been for some time two schools. Cartmel Grammar School was "an admirable institution" notes a Directory in 1876. Here in 1892 boarders were received for moderate fees and boys prepared for "any examinations with fees of £6" for "the usual course of English education – divinity, mathematics, Latin and French". The Cartmel National School (which was set up in 1861) at this time had about 70 scholars. The only Cartmel scholar of any note was Edmund Law who came from Staveley and went to St John's Cambridge, doubtless aided by the fund which Thomas Preston had left for this purpose. There he had a distinguished career after which from 1769 until his death in 1787 he was bishop of Carlisle.

South of the village, where the main roads of the area intersect is Headless Cross of which the present head is a modern restoration, but one or two of the stones on which it rests are ancient. Like the neighbouring crosses it may well have been broken up by the Roundheads who visited Cartmel in 1643.

In the years preceding World War I the charms of Cartmel attracted for holidays various literary figures including Edward Thomas, Gordon Bottomley (whose poem "Cartmel Bells" became well known) and Arthur Ransome who, as he relates in his autobiography, in 1905 stayed for the first time at Wallnook where Gordon Bottomley, who was living at Well Knowe, found him lodgings. At "the Flags" Arthur had, as he puts it, "a pack of cousins", amongst whom was the present writer's mother, whose attractiveness made her one of the somewhat limited number of his relations of whom he much approved; both agreed that the stories with which

Plate 13a — Canon Winder Hall, on the shore below Flookburgh.

Plate 13b — The earliest known picture of Holker Hall, from the Lonsdale Magazine of 1820.

Secret and Family
PRAYERS
With brief Helps for the more Devout
RECEIVING
OF THE
Lords-Supper.

And better Observation of the LORDS-DAY, as also to further the needfull Duties of Catechizing, Visiting the Sick, and Personal Instruction.

Fitted for the Use and Benefit of the Inhabitants of *Cartmel* in *Lancashire*.

If ye know these things, happy are ye if ye do them, S. John 13. 17.

CAMBRIDGE;
Printed by J. Hayes, for the Author. 1677.

Plate 14a — Title page of Rev J. Armstrong's prayer book for the parishioners of Cartmel.

CARTMEL, 1819.

ASSOCIATION
FOR THE
Prosecution of Poachers,
AND
UNQUALIFIED PERSONS;
AND FOR THE
Preservation of Game.

WHEREAS the GAME of every Kind in this NEIGHBOURHOOD, has been of late Years much DESTROYED, by POACHERS and other UNQUALIFIED PERSONS, who have been encouraged in their Practices by Higglers, Chapmen, and Carriers, and particularly by the Drivers of Stage Coaches, who unlawfully buy and sell Game so destroyed:

This is to give NOTICE,

That an Association has been formed of the Gentlemen whose Names are underwritten, being Owners of Manors and Lands in this Neighbourhood, who have mutually agreed to exert their utmost Endeavours to detect all such Offenders, and to Prosecute them at their joint Expense, with the utmost Severity of the Law.

And NOTICE is further given,

That all Persons giving such Information as shall lead to the Discovery and Conviction of any Poacher or unqualified Person, for using Dogs, Guns, Nets, Snares, or other Engine, for the Destruction of Game; or any Higgler, Chapman, Carrier, or Driver of any Coach, for unlawfully buying and selling the same, shall be entitled to a

Reward of TEN GUINEAS,

On Application to Mr. BARTON, Attorney at Law, in Cartmel, Clerk and Treasurer to the Association.

LORD GEO. CAVENDISH,	WILLIAM TOWNLEY,
GRAY RIGGE,	JOHN HARRISON,
THOS. M. MACHELL,	JAMES ADAM;
RD. MACHELL,	GEORGE BIGLAND, jun.

J. G. BARTON, Clerk and Treasurer.

Printed by W. Kendrew, Great John-Street, Ulverston.

Plate 14b — Poster 1819.

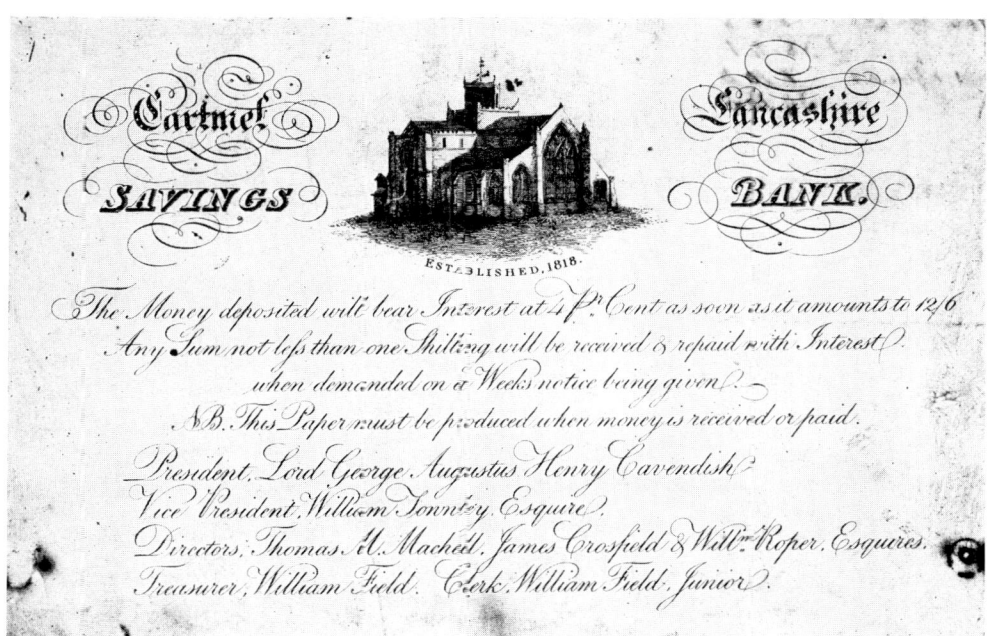

Plate 15a — Certificate of Cartmel Savings Bank.

Plate 15b — The Big Mill, Cark, built 1785 destroyed by fire 1936.

To be LET or SOLD,

BY PRIVATE TREATY,

AND ENTERED UPON IMMEDIATELY;

ALL THAT WELL-BUILT COMMODIOUS

Dwelling-house,

SITUATE AT GRANGE,

IN THE PARISH OF CARTMEL AND COUNTY OF LANCASTER,

late in the Possession of John Moreland, *Esq.*

CONSISTING of a Dining-Room, two Parlours, a large Kitchen, Pantry, Brew-house, two Cellars on the First-floor, two Stair-cases, seven Lodging-Rooms and Closets on the Second-floor, a large Room in the Attic which may be converted into two or three Lodging-Rooms, a large Cistern supplying the House with Rain-water, and a Pump near the Door, an useful Garden and valuable Orchard bearing excellent Fruit, a good Stable, Cow-house, two Coach-houses, Barn and other suitable Out-buildings.

These Premises adjoin to the Sea-shore and command a grand and extensive view of the whole Bay and opposite Country, remarkable for an excellent Bathing place, Vessels are frequently sailing under the Windows to and from *Liverpool, Glasgow,* &c. &c. five Miles from the Lake of *Windermere,* and two from *Cartmel Spaw.*

Mr. *B. Schrogham,* Cabinet-Maker, *Grange,* will shew the Premises, and for further Particulars Apply to *Mr. Gardner,* of *Cartmel.*

CARTMEL, JUNE 4th, 1811.

(J. Soulby, Ulverston, Print.)

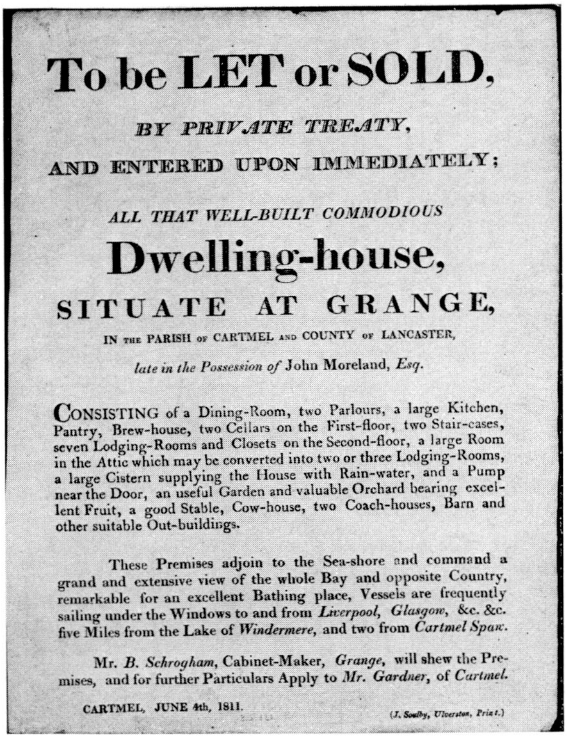

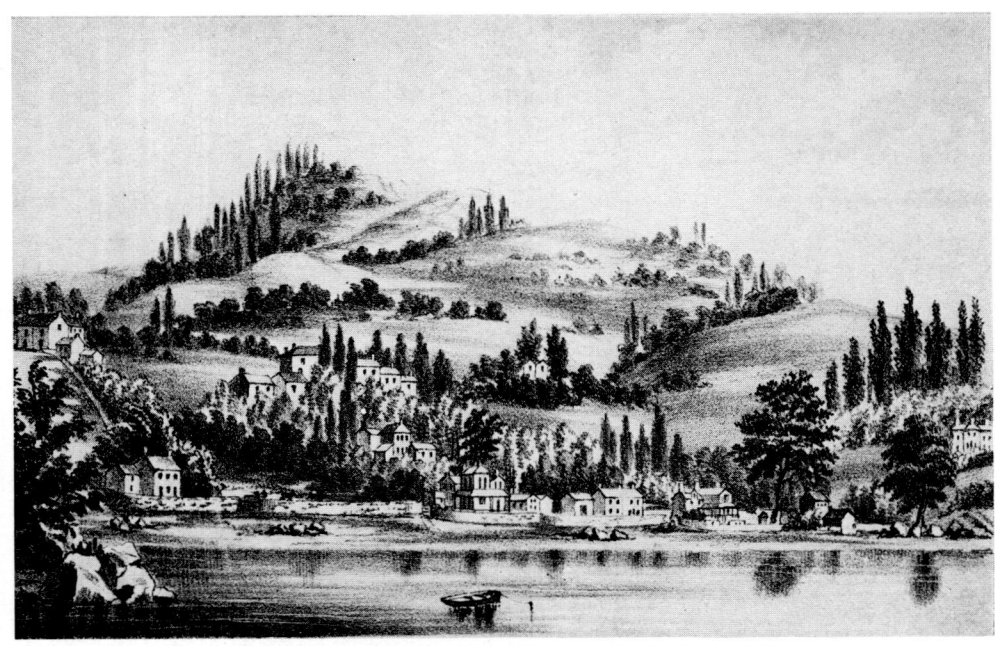

Plate 16a —
Notice of house at Grange, 1811.

Plate 16b — Early Grange (from a guide book *c.* 1850).

he now was wont to regale her could only be fully savoured by being recounted in the coalshed of her mother's house! In Windermere lurked the most Victorian of Victorian aunts who termed Arthur "the undesirable cousin" a title which delighted him hugely and led him to adopt the nickname of "the U.C.". His autobiography relates how, on New Year's Eve 1927, he and his wife "stood on the fell above the cottage (at Ludderburn) hearing at midnight the bells of Cartmel . . . with the snow deep under our feet": in 1931 they listened to them once again.

Cock-fighting survived in Lakeland and its environs long after it was officially dead. In Cartmel it is said to have gone on surreptitiously between the wars and for it cocks were bred. One such was given to a local lad who kept bantams, the donor remarking "It's na good, it waint fight!" The old cock-pit used in days when cock-fighting was not illegal was on the little eminence just beyond the entrance to Cartmel Park. From an unknown date, perhaps the time of Sir William Lowther, horse races have been held in the Park, Whit Monday being their traditional date, proceedings being officially organized since about the opening years of this century. Unhappily in very recent years what was a very charming little park has been largely marred by establishing therein unsightly racing paraphernalia, notably a circuit of glaring white railings, and an ungainly stand. Beyond the park lies Walton Hall whose name, as we have seen, is inscribed in *Domesday Book* (the original settlement was in a plantation some little distance away). The existing farmhouse may well retain some medieval walling and is certainly far from modern. In the seventeenth century we have reference to there being a hamlet at Walton of which there is now next to no trace. The waterfall nearby formerly ran a mill (see p. 55).

A little way north of Churchtown just off the road to Newton and Newby Bridge is Aynsome which consists largely of a house and a mill. The name is an old one meaning "at the lonely houses" which indirectly suggests strongly that there was nothing on the site of Cartmel when, in early times, this title was brought into use. As we have seen the mill is one of the oldest in Cartmel and was almost certainly constructed by the priory for the use of its members, dependants and tenants in the early thirteenth century. The house, also certainly originally a small farm, was done up by Thomas Michaelson Machell and is one of the local gentry's residences illustrated in the *Lonsdale Magazine* (1820); his additions included the large dining room which he termed "the royal room" on the grounds that the Duke and Duchess of Devonshire were wont to dine with him here!

Cartmel Fell

Cartmel Fell has no village and houses there are few, though one or two of these are substantial. No part of Cartmel valley is more secluded or has more delightful scenery, notably in the spring and autumn.

The major relic of antiquity is the picturesque chapel of St Anthony (Pl. 7b) enchantingly set in a charming little churchyard which looks across the unspoilt Winster valley to the mighty crag of Whitbarrow, and which in spring is adorned with hundreds of exquisite wild daffodils of most delicate hue. In the fifteenth century this area was studded with farms whose owners prospered not a little through the production of the wool. Amongst them were the well-to-do and pious Briggs family who lived at Swallowmire. Evidently just before 1504 one Robert Briggs and others built here the first chapel, whereat the local faithful could hear mass without involving themselves in the very exacting journey to Cartmel priory, along tracks which were often rank bad in weather which could be very hostile. It was a small, low rectangular building, with an unobtrusive tower at its west end lit by rectangular windows whose lights have simple semi-circular heads with no tracery. Very soon after its creation two small extensions were added on the north and south sides of the east end. The former had two storeys and may have been used to provide accommodation for the visiting celebrant of mass whether he was an Austin canon of Cartmel priory or a secular priest. The chapel was inevitably far from richly endowed, serving a scanty and much scattered population both before and after the Reformation.

Its interior was mercifully spared the crude wrecking of the Puritans.[16] The place avoided also the over-zealous "restoration" of the Victorians, with the result that it retains a great deal of its original furnishings. Most remarkable is the rather battered but still beautiful wooden crucifix (Pl. 8a), which is one of the very few such things of pre-Reformation date, still to be found in England. It is almost certainly contemporary with the chapel, i.e. dating to about 1500 and may have been placed above the now vanished rood screen. The figure is of oak and measures 80·5 cm (2′ 6″) long. It has unhappily lost both arms and its foot is charred, because, according to local tradition at one time it was used as a poker. In the last century for a time it was kept in the vicarage but later moved to a small case in the vestry. Very recently it was put in the charge of the Abbot Hall Museum for examination and restoration which was organized by Mr A. Behrens; examination with the latest scientific techniques included a photograph of a morsel of paint magnified 110 times! Though very little of the original colouring is still preserved, it is clear that the figure was largely painted in flesh colour with the wounds in scarlet and the crown and loin-cloth in gold. In view of the high interest of the figure, of which comparable surviving ones are so very rare, and the difficulty of keeping it in prime condition in the church to which it belonged, the authorities of the latter have sagely deposited it on loan in the Station Road Museum at Kendal.

Also very well worthy of note is the very interesting pre-Reformation glass in the chapel, notably that in the east window. The major and central part of this consists of extensive remains of a representation of Christ crucified with red rays from His seven wounds leading to adjacent panels depicting the Seven Sacraments of the Church. Unhappily the latter are far from intact. Those showing Baptism and Confirmation have totally disappeared along with most of those of Confession and Holy Unction. But very substantial remains of Ordination (Pl. 8c) and Marriage are still to be seen, and the panel showing the Mass (Pl. 8b) is very nearly intact and

---

[16] In a Cromwellian survey it is noted gloomily that chapel was served by "an old malignant not yet reconciled" who may well have been mainly responsible for saving much of its furnishings from destruction.

full of interest for the liturgical historian. The tonsured priest in a red chasuble kneels by the altar at the moment of elevation of the Elements, whilst nearby a small figure of the crucified Christ is included, as a reminder of His Real Presence in the Sacrament. Furnishings of the sanctuary are clearly shown and include the three flasks containing oil blessed by the bishop for liturgical purposes. Most of the rest of the glass here, like that in the adjacent window in the north wall, is probably of fifteenth century date and may well have been brought here from Cartmel priory at the Dissolution of the Monasteries. Of other glass in the east window the major items are figures of St Anthony of Egypt (the patron saint of the Chapel) with his emblem, a pig, close at hand and a similar one of St Leonard. At the bottom of the window are fragments of an inscription commemorating donors (members of the Briggs family) and asking for prayers for their souls.

Towards the east end of the nave, on opposite sides of it are two old family pews. That on the north side is much older than most of such things, dating from the early sixteenth century and belonging to Cowmire Hall. It retains various pre-Reformation remains, like the M and J on its frieze (standing for Mary and Jesus), and panels formerly painted with figures of saints. The other one, belonging to Burblethwaite Hall, is Jacobean. Close to it is one of the "three decker" pulpits so much in vogue in Anglican churches in the seventeenth and eighteenth centuries; it is dated 1698. The font is a small and simple circular one of eighteenth century date. A very unusual feature of the exterior of the church is the long stone bench built against its south wall. No doubt in this remote area where often time-keeping was difficult and roads often appalling, punctuality was a thing not easily achieved. The mounting block is a feature by no means without parallel in these parts, though the number of faithful who were accustomed to ride to church cannot have been at all large.

Although strictly speaking this work has no concern with the present antiquities of what used to be the county of Westmorland, it seems fruitful to draw attention at this point to the fact that not far from Cartmel Fell some more interesting stained glass from Cartmel priory is to be seen, in the great east window of Bowness parish church. This building is known to have been totally destroyed by fire, the consecration of the new edifice on the site by the bishop of Dromore having been authorised by the archbishop of York on 13 December 1483. Some of the existing glass in the east window was made for the new church about 1520. To this category belongs the large picture of the Crucifixion of Christ which fills much of the central lights of the window, and probably also the large royal coat of arms in the centre of the tracery above it and possibly some at least of the panels of donors at the bottom of the window which includes an attractive one of Sir William Thornburgh and his wyf (Pl. 9a).

But the rest of it is earlier (mostly fifteenth century), and certainly comes from Cartmel priory, doubtless purchased at cut rates for the newish church at Bowness at the time of the Dissolution of the Monasteries (1536-40). To this category belong the very extensive collection of the coats of arms of local families to be seen in the upper part of the window, which seem mainly to belong to the second quarter of the fifteenth century and may mostly have originally been in the cloister of the priory. Much more interesting than these are some of the large panels at the base of the lights of the east window. These both formerly had inscriptions which time has damaged, but were happily recorded for us by a seventeenth-century antiquary, Thomas Machell, whose voluminous notes on local history have happily survived. One of these shows "Willm. Plo . . . prior of Cartmel" kneeling in prayer (Pl. 9b); unfortunately no other mention of him has survived so we do not know the dates of his term of office. Very attractive is another one nearby which shows a group of Austin canons kneeling, each having a label attached to his mouth which originally gave his full name. According to Stockdale these are Thomas Hogson; Willym Baraye (Barrow); Willm. Purfoot; Roger Thwaites; George Fis . . .; all of these but the third are well-established local names. In the higher part of the window are to be seen a very small panel showing Our Lady, probably of late thirteenth century date, two examples of the coats of arms of Cartmel priory and an elaborate quartered coat of Lord Grey of Ruthyn (d. 1440), who had inherited the office of patron of the priory.

Flookburgh

The first element of its name may be derived from a person who delighted in the name of Floki, but it is at least equally likely that it comes from flukes, a quite tasty flat fish which until recently abounded in the coastal waters nearby. It is to be remembered that until the enclosures of the nineteenth century (see pp. 63-4) Flookburgh was in effect on the coast (Pl. 5) and that it was almost certainly in origin a collection of fishermens' huts.

Until the rise of Grange in the last hundred years or so Cartmel was mercifully free of anything that remotely resembled a town. The only place that was more than a small village was Flookburgh though to regard it as a borough in the modern sense is misleading, since it has never had more than a single street of importance and its population has never numbered more than a hundred or two. However it was something of a market centre largely because, as we have seen, it was situated on the major route which connected Lancaster with Furness and south Cumberland.

It is not surprising that the first dependent chapel of Cartmel priory was founded at Flookburgh, probably in the early thirteenth century,[17] though its origins and early history are very obscure indeed. It was a very small building and stood in the square in the centre of the village, which owes its present considerable size to the fact that it includes the site of the fairly extensive churchyard here which was removed about 1920 when circumstances had rendered it unnecessary, the old church having disappeared long before. The chapel for very long before and after the Reformation had no endowment. In 1650 it had "neither Minister nor maintenance, there being one hundred twenty families who humbly pray that it may be made a parish". But nothing was done then and it only became a parish in 1879. Meanwhile the ancient

[17] A voussoir of this date till recently visible in the church is likely to have come from the chapel.

building which probably retained some medieval work was with some difficulty replaced by a new one in 1776-7, as Stockdale describes in detail. The new edifice was a mere 60 feet by 30 feet wide within the wall and stone for it was to be got on Holker Bank, Wartbarrow or any other sound blue or limestone quarry. Stockdale, whose standards in this sort of thing may not have been very high, writes of the chapel as "of plain appearance and little like the ordinary church". Lady Frederick Cavendish, sensitive and deeply pious, was more downright. On 15 September 1872 she wrote in her diary "the horrible chapel sat upon me more than usual ... a mean conventicle is almost unbearable. It insults the Majesty of God!". Sometime afterwards came the desired change. On 4 December 1897 Lady Evelyn Cavendish laid the foundation stone of a new church on a very attractive site outside the village. On 20 October 1900 the new church – given by Victor Cavendish M.P. – was consecrated by the bishop of Carlisle. "The weather was splendid" notes Nash "and though the church was crowded to excess hundreds had to be turned away, there not even being room to seat all the specially invited clergymen". The architects were Austin and Paley and it is generally agreed that their work is singularly attractive, with early Gothic feeling but no pedantic imitation.

As we have seen, in pre-Railway days, the main route to Furness from Lancaster passed through Flookburgh, medieval travellers thereon including the future King Edward I and later ones John Wesley. But the traffic was certainly never enormous. Whether the prior of Cartmel held a market here is not certain but the Duke of Clarence, younger son of Henry IV, acquired a royal charter for a market here every Tuesday along with two annual fairs of three days each at Midsummer and Michaelmas. To what extent this privilege was effectively used is not known. This was confirmed by Charles II in a charter which still survives in excellent condition and is at present kept in the parish church (App. II). The smallness of Flookburgh perhaps partly explains why it is sometimes called a manor and not a borough, and there is certainly no signs of a flourishing civic life though a little regalia survives. In the Bodleian library are two court books of the manors of Cartmel and Flookburgh of late Tudor origin – MSS Rawlinson B343, 344: they cover the period 1591 to 1615 and contain much interesting information on local social life. In 1602 it was presented that "noe men nor boyes in this liberty shall play at the hand ball or fote ball in the chapel yard or anye part of the more", and most inhabitants were also not to "bowle or use bowling within the libertie or any parte of the more". Even today Flookburgh has little more than the one long road – Main Street – which leads westward to Sandgate where the crossing into Furness began. On a wall of the farm on the righthand side of the road at this point there remained until World War II a large and interesting notice (probably of late eighteenth or early nineteenth century date) giving instructions to members of the general public on how to establish contact with the guide from Ulverston; their main concern was to make towards a white house on the opposite shore, which is now no longer visible.

Flookburgh has suffered what were by local standards two major catastrophes. The parish registers of Lakeland show that not infrequently in the sixteenth and seventeenth centuries there were outbreaks of what was hazily called "plague" which sometimes took very heavy toll of the population. A very violent one ravaged Flookburgh, possibly in 1598 or 1665, and evidently led to the dead being buried in mass graves in Eccleston Meadow. "In or about 1686" according to Stockdale, came a fire which certainly caused such very great damage that the Crown was officially petitioned to authorise an official collection towards "the rebuilding of the towne" and very heavy losses to "household goods, corne, graine, maulte, bedinge, bedsteads and other goods, amounting in the whole to the value of three thousand pounds and upwards", twenty-two houses, besides barns, stables, kilns and outhouses.

Most of the houses in Flookburgh are small and very few can be dated, though some retain very ancient timber including, Mr A. Frearson informs me, some former ships' masts. The house at the west end of the main street with a date-stone of 1686 is called the Manor House and is believed to have been held for some time by the stewards of the manor. Near it are two small hotels on the other side of the street which are thought to have been built largely for visitors to the Holy Well at Humphrey Head. Halfway up the hill at the other end of the street is a house with the date-stone 1654 built by one of the Braithwaite family who were by local standards wealthy at this time; unhappily between the wars its windows lost its attractive mullions.

The low lands below the village were, as we have seen, largely reclaimed early in the last century. Their isolation, flatness and accessibility to the railway (a halt was established at Wraysholme for a time) led to part of it being used for military training. The army was here in World War I, towards the end of which was erected here an enormous wooden structure to provide moorings for airships which was never used. In World War II the R.A.F. practised night-flying here as locals became very much aware. To the west on higher ground came into existence the place called Ravenstown with streets called after First World War battles including Jutland, which for a while gave the place an alternative name. It is small with purely domestic buildings. The area below Jutland is known as Winder – "the shelter against the wind" – and from medieval times was divided into two estates – Raven Winder called after someone with Scandinavian blood in his veins, and Canon Winder so-called because it came to belong to the canons of Cartmel priory. Both retain halls of great antiquity, Raven Winder has been extensively altered and has little to show. Canon Winder Hall (Pl. 13a), on the other hand, has a very handsome front facing the nearby sea shore with mullioned windows, the lower ones being large, and having transoms as well as two doors. Some work may be quite early but most belongs to about the very late seventeenth century. In front of the house is a grass court which has on its western side an attractive entrance having stone piers crowned by ball ornaments. It never became a family seat for long, its most notable owner being Thomas Walton who got into much trouble through being involved in the 1715 Jacobite rebellion.

Grange-over-Sands

"Grange" is a quite common place-name as it denotes what was in later medieval England a quite common thing – a farm, often quite sizable, owned and run by a monastery, to help supply its own needs. Sometimes these were quite small, like those which Cartmel priory had at Silverdale and Frith, but others, especially those of the Cistercians, like those of Furness abbey at Hawkshead and Borrowdale, were quite sizable. As we have seen Cartmel had a grange which gave Grange-over-Sands the first part of its name, the second part being added in Victorian times when it was suggested by the local vicar so as to prevent the place being confused with its namesake in Borrowdale. In the early parish registers of Cartmel sometimes references were made to the place as "the Grange", a usage which gradually became extinct.

There is not the slightest doubt that down to very recent centuries Grange attracted next to no mention in official documents for the very simple reason that the number of its inhabitants was miniscule. Why was this? To such a question geology and geography between them provide most of the answer. The fact that the slopes on which Grange is situate are not only steep, but consist largely of rock and provide next to no water supply meant that no farmer would try to make a living here and that, despite its noble scenery, it had no great attraction for private residences until such things as piped water had been provided.

Nothing is more difficult than to visualise the early layout of Grange, partly because documentary references to it are so scanty, but also because modern alterations (principally those connected with the construction of the railway station and its adjacent embankments) have destroyed or buried too deep for us to examine what is almost certainly interesting archaeological evidence. Careful study, however, does suffice to show that there was in this area what was from the local angle, a most important feature, to wit a pool in which shipping could sail at least at high water and wherein they could obtain safe anchorage. There seems originally to have been on the land side of the railway a longish ridge of rock separating the sea from a narrow channel much of which is now covered by the pond of the ornamental gardens, and which continued on towards the old road to Eggerslack and Lindale where it probably twisted to form a pool (below the Grange Hotel) whose existence an early guide-book shows us. (It is possible that the pool came up as far as the area which until fairly recently were used as tennis courts, *inter alia* for annual tournaments which have been claimed to be the second oldest of their kind in England.)

If a historian may indulge in geological speculation, this pool and the channel leading up to it had been scooped out over the centuries by the relentless pressure of the "bore", which was long very evident here as it still is in the Severn. In this connection it is most interesting to note, as Ekwall does not, that this spot is known as Eggerslack, the second element of which means "a hollow in the ground"; the first (*egor*) denoting "flood, high tide" is very rare indeed, but is used to refer to the Trent Bore. It is very likely indeed that this pool was used in Roman times. As we have seen (p. 4), an early medieval charter suggests that there was a Roman road in this area; there was certainly a Roman site of some kind at Castlehead not far away, whilst Roman coins have been found at Merlewood just up the road from the former pool.

Once Cartmel priory had been established it needed a small harbour for effective conduct of its affairs, such as its links with its property in Ireland, the need for brethren to go to and from their cell at Silverdale, and their visits to Lancaster on business and even further afield in England (like those to the General Chapters of their order). That their harbour for all this was at Grange there is no doubt at all. A good dry road linked it with the priory and its use continued when the monastery had gone. In 1598 we find the *Church Book* of Cartmel noting the purchase of "12 tunns of sea coales be bought beinge then at Grange".

What did the original Grange look like? There was certainly a little quay or possibly merely a jetty alongside which the small craft which were all that could be accommodated, could berth. But the main feature was almost certainly a large barn which could be used for temporary or permanent storage alongside which would be some smaller structures. These may well have long survived the suppression of the priory that built them. The old barn is possibly shown in one of the pictures of early Grange in a sketch book (whose present whereabouts is unknown) from which they were reproduced in A. M. Wakefield's *A Haunt of Ancient Peace*, whose description of Grange in the early decades of the last century is easily the best thing in the book. The building probably stood alongside the vanished pool opposite the station. There can be no doubt that after the disappearance of the priory maritime activity at Grange shrank to very small proportions, there now being no major local demand for it, though understandably some mariners seem to have dwelt in the area.

As a picture of Grange in an admirable guidebook to the area published in 1850 shows clearly (Pl. 16b) even at this date buildings here were decidedly sparse by modern standards and they so remained for a few decades to come. A map of the place of 1879 shows that even then dwellings along the whole length of the one main street which Geography allowed Grange to have, were very few, and side streets crammed with dwellings were non-existent. (A directory of 1849 made very brief mention of "the village of Grange" noting little except that it had a Sunday school set up in 1811 which became a day school in 1832.)

However the immense beauty of the surroundings at Grange and the mildness of its climate (which won it the title of "the Torquay of the North") meant that its future as a residential area was assured once these were known and easy access became available. It is interesting to note that we have some slight but significant signs of tourist development quite early in the nineteenth century. About this time an extremely elaborate mansion was built down by the shore, where on occasion at least the channel swept close by, in pre-railway days. The attractions of the place, enumerated in a poster (Pl. 16a) advertising it are most extensively included having ships to Liverpool and Glasgow passing nearby.

The Crown Hotel at the top of the hill to which it now gives its name, was probably established about the same time. It is quite likely that a main motive behind the establishment of these places to accommodate visitors drawn here by the popularity then enjoyed by Holy Well at Humphrey Head (see pp. 71-2). The *History*,

Directory and Gazetteer of Lancashire of 1824 notes that its waters were "celebrated as a remedy for stone, gout and cutaneous complaints" and that "its medicinal qualities occasion a considerable influx of company to Cartmel, Flookburgh, Kents Bank and Grange during the summer months".

But it was certainly the railway which made Grange, even if its growth was quite slow until the dawn of the present century. The station built here (in 1857) was more than usually elaborate, as comparison with those of Kents Bank and Arnside shows us, not as at Cark because of local grandees, but for tourists. Very significantly with its construction was linked that of the Grange Hotel, which was much the most elaborate structure of the kind that locals had yet seen and attracted no little applause. A Directory of 1876 terms Grange "this delightful and fashionable watering place" and mentions "A splendid Hotel in the Italian style of architecture (!) . . . opened in 1866, having 70 rooms also large refreshment rooms, stables, etc. Swimming and other baths are fitted up and supplied with sea water"; in front of it were "extensive pleasure grounds, in the centre of which is a fresh water lake".

Victorian England being as pious as it was, it is not surprising that in these times when Allithwaite, Broughton and Flookburgh acquired new churches, a place of worship should be built at Grange, to prevent the necessity of having recourse to Cartmel or Lindale on the Lord's Day. This church, dedicated to St Paul was built in 1853 and acquired its own parish in 1884. A Wesleyan chapel followed in 1874-5, a small Roman Catholic one in 1884 and a Congregational chapel in 1899. A school was erected in 1864 and was extensively enlarged in 1886 in which year the Gas Works were established at Meathop. Previously in 1877 a water supply from Newton had been secured. The Promenade was constructed in 1902-4 "measuring in some parts 60 feet across". On 1 January 1901 as Nash reports "the New Hall at Grange opened by Miss Little"; Miss Wakefield commenced her lecture on "North Country Songs" but broke down owing to the smell of new paint, so the meeting ended with "a lot of speeches and much complimenting all round". Behind these developments lay a rise in population which was steady if not spectacular. In 1851, it was estimated, Grange had 260 people and 70 houses. In 1871 over 200 houses and 1200 people, in 1891 – 1733 people. In 1874 Grange was made the centre of a Local Board.

Lindale

The name of Lindale in Cartmel like that of its name-sake Lindal in Furness (the difference in spelling is modern) indicates a place with lime trees. Geography made Lindale a small place, setting it on a rocky slope with much marshland below and very poor communications for most of its history. Until the great road of 1822 brought life to it (which is being much intensified by the great motor road now in construction in the area) Lindale's communications by land was very poor, whilst the access to the waters of the bay which it had up to the time of the construction of the railway and its embankment, did not attract major maritime activity.

As we have seen, however, it is at Castlehead just outside the village and only at Castlehead that we have indications of a Roman site of some little importance in the land of Cartmel. It is likely that this place continued in some sort of use in Viking times, but there is nothing to indicate that it was anything more than a ruin in the days when the monastic life flourished at Cartmel priory.

Rather unexpectedly, as we have seen, the place took on a new lease of life in the eighteenth century through the settlement in the area of Isaac and John Wilkinson (see p. 55). As we have seen, he built for himself a typically ostentatious house at Castlehead in the course of the construction of which no few interesting archaeological objects were discovered. Until the coming of the railway and its embankment the waters of the bay ran near the house and went on inland to the bottom of the village of Lindale. A little further on was Wilson House where Wilkinson had worked in his early days.

After his death the body of Wilkinson (who was certainly much more of a freethinker than was thought desirable in those days) was brought to Lindale in an iron coffin to be buried in the grounds as he desired. He had prepared a not unattractive memorial to himself – a massive pillar of iron having a large medallion of his head (saved from removal for salvage during World War II by a local who deserves no little gratitude) and a longish inscription which tells us "his different works in various parts of the kingdom are lasting testimony of his unceasing labours. His life was spent in action for the benefit of man, as, as he presumed humbly to hope, to the glory of God". Few mens' bones had so complex a process of burial. On their way to the burial at Castlehead which John Wilkinson had ordered, they were for a while detained by the sands near Holme Island. But the grave prepared for the coffin in the ground of his house proved too small for it, so his remains were given a temporary burial here until a larger coffin (of iron as he had ordered) was made. But it was found that solid rock prevented adequate enlargement of the grave for it, so another temporary burial followed. Burial in the grounds was finally effected and the huge iron pillar (weighing 20 tons) erected on top of it. In 1828 the Castlehead house and grounds were put up for auction and once again Wilkinson's mortal remains were exhumed, to receive their final burial at dead of night although local tradition to this day differs as to whether it was in the church or in the churchyard or in unconsecrated ground just outside of the then existing boundaries of the latter. So do the glories of this world depart!

Down to very modern times the folk of Lindale, like those of Staveley, Cartmel and Flookburgh were far too few and unplutocratic to be able either to provide themselves with a notable place of worship or to produce a salary adequate for a full-time incumbent. It is unlikely that they had their own place of worship in medieval times and certain that hitherto no mention of it, is earlier than 1617 in which year there was a "reader". Not long after the interesting Commonwealth Survey of the local churches (1650) claims there were 120 families here as against 128 at Flookburgh and tells us that the chapel at Lindale "hath neither Minister nor Maintenance though the same be a place of great necessity for both". A report made in 1708 shows shocking neglect, Holy Communion was never administered there, the altar was not railed in and there was no surplice, such services as there were being taken by a reader. Not long afterwards the chapel was in need of repair, and a brief for this obtained. An old print of this chapel happily survives (Pl. 11a) and shows a very small and simple building with windows not unlike those of Cartmel Fell chapel, though they may be appreciably later in date.

A small new church replaced this in 1828, being consecrated the following year and acquiring a chancel in 1864 through public subscriptions (there being no very well-to-do family in the parish), the parsonage having been enlarged four years before.

APPENDIX I

I

The foundation charter of Cartmel Priory

The original foundation charter of Cartmel Priory has perished with almost all the other archives of the monastery, but an official copy of it (along with a few minor allied texts) survives and has been printed in W. Farrer's *The Lancashire Pipe Rolls* (Liverpool, 1902), pp. 343-4, of which a translation is here given.

To all the sons of holy mother church to whom the present writing shall come William Marshall (sends) greeting. Know you all that in order to spread the cultivation of the holy monastic life I have given and conceded in free, unconditional and perpetual alms to God and to His most Holy mother Mary and to the canons there serving God, all my land of Kertmel with all its appurtenances, for the soul of the lord King Henry the Second and for the soul of the younger King Henry and for the soul of King Richard and for my soul and the soul of my wife Isabel and for the souls of our ancestors, successors and heirs. I have also given to them and conceded with equal devout desire the church of the same land with all its chapels and all its advowsons and with everything pertaining to them. Where I desire and firmly order that the aforesaid canons have and hold all the aforesaid land of Kertmel for ever, free and peaceful with all its appurtenances in churches and chapels, in woodland and in plain, in forest and in hunting rights, in roads and paths, in meadowland and in pasturage, in the sea and in all waters and mills, in grazing and in fishing, in iron mines and in all other things and places, with all their liberties and free customs, freely and quietly, wholly and with honour.

Further I wish and enjoin that the aforesaid house and the canons there serving God shall be free and immune of all subjection to another house and that they shall not be in a position of subjection to any other house, but obeying the prior of the aforesaid place of Kertmel. The canons shall choose two canons and present them to me William Marshall their patron or my heirs, in order that he whom our common assent has selected, be made prior, in such a way that whoever is established as prior there shall always have such name and office of Prior, and so that the priory shall never be made an abbey. This house, moreover I have founded for the increase of holy monasticism, giving and conceding to it whatever freedom the mount can utter or the heart of man conceive. Whosoever, therefore shall inflict damage or detriment to the aforesaid house or its belongings will incur the curse of God and of the most blessed Virgin Mary and of all the saints of God and of myself. Wherefore so that this my donation be valid in the present and remain undamaged by posterity, I have fortified this present writing with the impress of my seal, these being witnesses – William Earl of Salisbury; John, marshal of the lord King, my brother; Geoffrey fitzPiers; Robert of Berkeley; Geoffrey fitzRobert; Richard of Mucegros; Ralph Bloet; Philip of Prendergast; John of Erley; William of St. Leger; Nicholas Avenell; Richard of Stutecumb; William Waleran; Philip of Salisbury; Roger the chaplain; Joceline, Michael and Pentecost clerks with many others.

(The date of the document is after 1189 and probably early in 1190.)

II

The foundation of a monastery in those times involved a fairly elaborate process including legal permission so to do by the founder's overlord, who in the case of Cartmel was no less a person than the future King John who was at the time Count of Mortain. His confirmation has survived and is here translated.

John, Count of Mortain, to all his friends and freemen, French and English greeting. Know that I have granted and confirmed by my present charter for the health of my soul and those of my ancestors that William Marshall may establish a house of whatever monastic order he desires in the land of Kertmel, and that he, William, may give to that house and to those who shall serve God there Kertmel with all its appurtenances, in perpetual alms, for the health of his souls and the souls of his ancestors, as freely and fully in all things as I myself granted, and by my charter confirmed it to the same William. Wherefore I wish and firmly order that the aforesaid religious of whatever monastic order they be shall have and hold the before-named land of Kertmel in free and full alms, with all its appurtenances and churches and chapels, in woodland and plain, in forest and hunting rights, in roads and paths, in meadows and pastures, in waters and mills, in herbage and fisheries, in salt pans and workshops with all liberties and free customs that pertain to the same land as freely and fully, honorably and completely as the charter of the donation the beforementioned William confirms to them and witnesses saving the service of one knight which is due from it to me to use from the same William.

Witnesses. Stephen Ridel, chancellor, William Avenell, Roger de Amundeville, William de Turberville and Ralph de Ardern.

(The date of deed is probably a little later in 1190 than that of the foundation charter.)

APPENDIX II

The charter of King Charles II concerning the holding of a market at Flookburgh (8 Dec. 1663)

    We Charles the Second of England, Scotland, France and Ireland King, Defender of the Faith. To all to whom these presents shall come greeting. We have inspected the enrolment of a certain Charter made by Lord Henry the fourth our Progenitor heretofore King of England and granted to his illustrious Son Thomas de Lancaster Duke of Lancaster and Clarence, enrolled among the Patent Rolls of the thirteenth year of this reign of the said King, and kept among the records of Chancery within our Tower of London in these words:— The King to the Archbishops, Bishops, Abbots, Priors, Dukes, Earls, Barons, Judges, Sheriffs, Mayors, Ministers, Bailiffs and all his faithful Subjects greeting. Know ye that we have granted by this our Charter have confirmed to our illustrious Son Thomas de Lancaster Duke of Clarence that he and his Heirs forever may hold a market upon Tuesday in every week within his manor of Flookburgh in the county of Lancaster, and also a fair yearly and every year at the same place to continue for three days viz. upon the eve of the nativity and upon the morrow of the nativity of Saint John the Baptist, and that he may hold one other fair yearly and every year at the place aforesaid to continue for three days, to wit upon the eve of the feast, upon the feast, and upon the morrow of the feast of Saint Michael the Archangel with all issues, tolls and amercements arising from markets and fairs of the like sort, together with all and every the profits, advantagements and emoluments belonging on in any manner appertaining to such markets and fairs, Provided this market and these be no detriment or disadvantage to other neighbouring markets and fairs. Wherefore our will is and we strictly enjoin for ourselves and for our heirs that the said Thomas and his heirs forever may be allowed to hold and keep the aforesaid market and fairs within his manner aforesaid with all libertys and free customs to markets and fairs of the like sort belonging, provided that this market and these fairs be no detriment or disadvantage to neighbouring markets and fairs as was aforesaid.

    . . . .

Given under the hand of the King at Westminster the 19th Day of July and We at the request of John Neesington Esquire have recited the aforesaid Charter with the rest of the premises therein contained exemplified by these presents. In Witness whereof we have caused these our Letters patent to be made patent Witness ourselves at Westminster the eighth day of December in the fifteenth Year of our reign.

APPENDIX III

The following most curious document has recently been discovered amongst some Rawlinson papers and I am greatly obliged to Mrs F. Suren for permission to print it here.

Copy of Paper belonging to Mrs Feronside, Poulton le Sands, March 30 1868
About the time of the disappearance of the "Iron Mask" a hauty reserved and extremely Gentlemanlike Foreigner came to reside in the neighbourhood of *Cark* in Lancashire – He would not visit with any of the Families around, but was visited once a year by the Duke of Somerset,[18] and it was observed that whenever they walked abroad, the Duke with Cap in Hand always opened the Doors and Gates for his Host the *Stranger* – The Rawlinsons of Cark Hall had a young cousin Kate Rawlinson, with their great aunt Eleanor Rawlinson on their annual visit; and one morning before Breakfast her cousin Christopher Rawlinson found her Slipper in a Hedge in the Grounds as he was rambling about; he took it with him into the Breakfast Room and told the party that he would have a jest with Kate about the slipper when she came down, as he knew it must be hers by its smallness – Kate however did not make her appearance – They became alarmed, scoured the Country round in quest of her and at last discovered that she had eloped with the Son of the *Stranger* – At first the family was enraged at the event but after a lapse of time relented, and Christopher called upon the *Stranger* and tendered assistance to the young Couple through the interests of the Rawlinsons at Court and in any other mode within their power; all of which were declined. The *Stranger* who assumed the name of Rigge used to tell his Son and his Wife that the name of Rigge was assumed but that before he died he would reveal to them his real Name – He frequently hinted that he was above all around him – When the Duke of Somerset came they were closeted for hours. He was taken ill and gathering his Family together he told them that the time was arrived and he would now reveal himself. His resolution failed him and he said "Better not yet", "Better not now". He died and his secret with him. As soon as he had breathed his last an express happened to arrive from the Duke of Somerset, the Courier immediately returned on hearing of the death of the *Stranger* without declaring to the Family the purport of his Mission. – This Circumstance was related to Mrs Heys (Mother to Mrs Sweltenham, the Countess of Winterton whose father was the only surviving Child of Kate and the Son of the Stranger, by her Aunts who were Coheiresses and who intended to make her their heiress).

The *Iron Mask* was *Twin* brother to Louis 14th King of France. He was imprisoned from Jealousy, as no one could tell which was the *eldest* Brother, but escaped and left the Country.

What do we make of this?

---

[18] Charles Seymour, 6th Duke of Somerset 1662-1748. Speaker of the Lords 1690; Joint regent 1701; enjoyed with his wife the confidence of Queen Anne; lost his place in council 1711.

APPENDIX IV

Obituary Notice of William Gibson from 'The Gentleman's Magazine', Nov. 1791.

1791 October 4th   At his house at Blawith near Cartmel occasioned by a fall he got in Eggerslack when returning from Cartmel, Mr William Gibson. He was born in the year 1720 At a village called Boulton, a few miles from Appleby in Westmorland. At the death of his father, being left young without parents or any immediate means of support he put himself under the care of a reputable farmer in the neighbourhood to learn the farming business where he remained several years. Having obtained some knowledge therein he removed to the distance of about 30 miles to be superintendant to a farm near Kendal. After being there some time and arrived at the age of 17 or 18, he was informed that his father had been possessed of a tolerable estate in landed property, and that in the beginning of the last century, he had descended from the same family with Dr Edmund Gibson then Bishop of London. He spent the little money he had acquired by his industry to come at the truth of the business: when he found to his sorrow that the estate was mortgaged to its full value, and upwards. He therefore continued his occupation, and soon afterwards rented and managed a little farm of his own, at a place called Hollins in Cartmelfell not far from Cartmel, where he applied himself vigorously in study. A little time previously to this he had admired the operation of figures; but laboured under every disadvantage for want of education. As he had not been taught either to read or write he turned his thoughts to reading English, and enabled himself to read and comprehend a plain Author. He therefore purchased a treatise on arithmetic, vulgar and decimal fractions, the extraction of the square and cube roots etc. by his memory only, and became so expert therein that he could tell without setting down a figure the product of any two numbers multiplied together; although the multiplier and the multiplicand, each of them consisted of nine places of figures; and it was equally astonishing how he could answer in the same manner, questions in division, in decimal fractions, or in the extraction of the square or cube roots, where such a multiplicity of figures is often required in the operation yet at this time he did not know that any merit was due to himself, conceiving other people's capacity like his own, but being a sociable companion, and when in company taking a particular pride in puzzling his companions with proposing different questions to them, they gave him others in return which from the certainty and expertitious manner he had in answering them, made him first noticed as an arithmetician and a man of most wonderful memory. Finding himself still labouring under further difficulties for want of a knowledge in writing he taught himself to write a tolerable hand. As he did not know the meaning of the word mathematicks, he had no idea of anything beyond what he had learned He thought himself a masterpiece in figures and challenged all his companions and the society he attended. Something however was proposed to him concerning Euclid; but as he did not understand the meaning of the word he was silent, but afterwards it means a book, containing the elements of Geometry which was purchased and applied himself very diligently to the study and against the next meeting, in this new science. He was proposed with an answer. He now found himself launching out into a field of which before he had no conception. He continued his

Geometrical studies and as the demonstration of the different propositions in Euclid depend entirely upon a recolection of some of those proceeding his memory was of the utmost service to him; and as it did not require much knowledge in classical education but principally the management of straight lines, it was a study just to his mind for while he was attending his business of the farm and humming over some tune or other with a sort of whistle, his attention was certain to be solely engaged upon some of his geometrical propositions and with the assistance of a piece of chalk upon the top of his breeches knee or any other convenient spot would clean up the most difficult parts of the science in a most masterly manner. His mind being now open a little to the works of nature, he paid particular attention to the theory of the earth the moon and the rest of the planets belonging to this system, of which the sun is the centre and considering the distance and magnitude of the different bodies belonging to it and the distance of the fixed stars, he soon conceived each to be the centre of a different system. He well considered the laws of gravity and that of the centripetal and centrifugal forces, and the cause of the ebbing and flowing of the tides, also the projection of the sphere stereographic, orthographic and gnomonical; also trigonometry and astronomy. He paid particular attention to and was never better pleased than when he found his calculations agree with observation and being well acquainted with the projection of the sphere he was fond of describing all astronomical questions geometrically and of projecting the eclipses of the Sun and Moon that way. By this time he was possessed of a small library. He next turned his thoughts to algebra and took up Emerson's treatise on that subject, and though the most difficult, and that with Simpson's are the best authors, yet published he went through it with great success and the management of such quantities, and the clearing of equations of high power were amusement to him while at work in the fields, as he could generally could perform them by his memory and if he met with anything very intricate he had recourse to a piece of chalk as in his geometrical propositions. The arithmetic of infinites and the differential method, he made himself master of, and found out that algebra and geometry were the very soul of the mathematicks. He therefore paid a particular attention to them, and used to apply the former to almost every branch of the different sciences. The art of Navigation the principales of mechanicks, also the doctrine of motion, of falling bodies, and the elements of optics, he grounded himself in, and as a preliminary to fluxions which had only been lately discovered by Sir Isaac Newton, as the boundary of the mathematicks, he went through conic sections to make a trial of this last and finishing branch though he expressed some difficulty at his first entrance yet he did not rest till he made himself master of both a fluxion and a flowing quantity. As he had paid a similar attention to all the intermediate parts, he was become so conversant in every branch of the mathematicks that no question was ever proposed to him that he did not answer, nor any rational question in the mathematicks that he ever thought of which he did not comprehend. He used to answer all the questions in the Gentlemen and Lady's Diaries, the Palladium and other annual publications for several years; but his answers were seldom inserted, except by or in the name of some other persons, for he had no ambition in making his abilities known farther than satisfying himself that nothing passed him which he did not understand. He frequently has had questions from his pupils and other gentlemen in London, the universities and different parts of the country as well as from the university of Gottingen in Germany sent him to solve, which he never failed to answer; and from the minute enquiry he made into natural philosophy there was scarcely a phenomenon in nature that ever came to his knowledge or observation but he could in some measure or other reasonably account for it.

He went by the name of Willy o'th' Hollins for many years after he left the place. He removed to Tarngreen where he lived about 15 years, and from thence into the neighbourhood of Cartmel and was best known by the name of Willy Gibson still continuing his occupation as before. For the last 40 years of his life he kept a school of about eight or ten gentlemen, who boarded and lodged at his house on his farm; and having a happy time of explaining his ideas, he had turned out a great many very able mathematicians, and a great many more gentlemen has he instructed in accompts for the counting house, as well as for the sea, and for land surveying which profession he followed himself for these last forty years and upwards. In the course of his life he had very great practice that way; and having acquired a little knowledge of drawing could finish plans in a very pretty manner. He has been several times appointed by acts of parliament a commissioner for the inclosing of commons, and was a very proper person for that purpose; for as well as his practice in land surveying, he had equal experience and judgement in the quality of land as well as the quantity; also in leveling or conveying of water from one place to another for he was well acquainted with the curvature of the earth's surface. He used to study incessantly during the greatest part of the night; and in the day time when in the fields his pupils frequently went to him to have their difficulties removed. He was fond of society and his company was courted by all who knew him. He has left a disconsolate widow to mourn for the loss of an indulgent and affectionate husband. They had been married and lived together in the purest harmony and friendship for near fifty years; and in all probability if it had not been for this or some other similar accident from their apparent health and constitution they might have lived together many years longer and before this melancholy accident he had never been out of health an hour in all his life. He has also left ten children living to lament the loss of a tender and indulgent parent. He was well known and respected by a numerous acquaintance, by several eminent gentlemen in the city of London and in other parts of the kingdom, and particularly so for a considerable distance around his place of residence. He had but four days illness; and though he was in the greatest agony from a bruise he had got in his inside by the fall, he bore it with the greatest patience, and died in the greatest composure, aged 71 years.

APPENDIX V

The Holker Charity School

Very little is known about this interesting little establishment apart from the *Rules* for it here printed from a copy from what must have been a small private edition. But the fact that its patroness was the Countess of Burlington suggests that the booklet belongs to the time of Lord George Augustus Henry Cavendish who was made Earl of Burlington in 1831, and held the Holker estates.

RULES

Rule I The education in this School shall be open to the children of such poor persons within the Parish of Cartmel, as are not in circumstances of life to enable them to bear the expense of procuring a suitable education for their children.

Rule II The Master and Mistress shall instruct the Boys and Girls in reading, writing, and in accounts, as far as the rule of Practice. The afternoon of Friday in each week shall be exclusively employed in repeating the Church Catechism, and in other religious instruction.

Rule III Such religious books and tracts, only, shall be introduced into the School as are contained in the Catalogue of the Society for promoting Christian Knowledge, or are recommended by the National Society.

Rule IV The hours of attendance in this School, shall be from nine o'clock until twelve, and from one o'clock until four throughout the year. Morning and Evening Prayers are to be said by one of the Scholars, the former before the business of the School commences, and the latter at its close, when the Evening Hymn will be sung.

Rule V The School-roll shall be called over every Sunday Morning and Afternoon, before Divine Service, when the children shall be arranged and conducted by the Master and Mistress to the Chapel of the Established Religion at Flookburgh. The same shall also be done on Christmas-Day and Good Friday.

Rule VI Each Scholar, who shall have punctually attended School Morning and Evening, and also on Sundays, at the appointed hours of attendance and behaved with perfect propriety throughout the day, shall at the close of that day receive one Ticket from the Master or Mistress, such Tickets to be valued as the Patroness may direct.

Rule VII That Scholar, who shall have risen to, or continued at the head of each class during the day, shall at the close of the day receive two additional Tickets, and that Scholar who then occupies the second place in each class, shall receive one additional Ticket.

Rule VIII The Master and Mistress shall select the Teachers of the different classes, and their assistants from the most attentive and deserving children; and these Teachers if they have performed their duties to the satisfaction of the Master or Mistress, shall as a reward for their attention receive three-pence each, and their Assistants two-pence each at the end of every week.

Rule IX The Minister of Flookburgh, the Minister of Cartmel, the Master of the Free Grammar School at Cartmel, with any others of the neighbouring Clergy, who may be disposed to give their assistance, and the Steward at Holker Hall, shall be appointed a Committee to visit the School on the last Friday in each month, at two o'clock in the afternoon, and shall then inspect the general state and discipline of the School, and the progress of the Scholars in learning, and at the close of each such Meeting, they shall enter in a book to be kept for that purpose, such remarks and observations, as the result of their examination may suggest.

Rule X The above-named Committee shall be empowered to give occasional leave of absence to the Scholars on such grounds as the Patroness may direct, such leave of absence to be in all cases asked by the Parents, and not by the Children themselves.

Rule XI If any Child be absent from School, either Morning or Afternoon, without leave obtained in writing from one of the members of the Visiting Committee, the Master and Mistress shall respectively register such cases of absence without leave, in books kept for that purpose.

Rule XII On the Wednesday immediately preceding each Monthly Meeting of the Committee, the Master and Mistress shall issue notices to the Parents or Friends of all such Children as shall have been absent from School without leave during the past month, desiring them to attend the Meeting of the Committee at the School, on the Friday following, when all cases of non-attendance shall be enquired into, and the Committee shall have power either to order the exclusion of such Children, or, after a suitable admonition, to permit their continuance in the School, according as the merits of the different cases may seem to require.

Rule XIII If the Parents or Friends, after notice sent to attend the Meeting of the Committee, shall wilfully neglect to attend to such notice, then the Committee shall have power to order the immediate expulsion of the Children of such persons from the School.

Rule XIV At each Monthly Meeting of the Committee, the Copy-books of the children will also be examined, when, to those Children who seem to have made the greatest progress in writing, and to have kept the neatest and most correct Copy-books, the following rewards will be given, viz.

HEAD CLASS		SECOND CLASS	
Best Copy-book	6 Tickets	Best Copy-book	3 Tickets
2nd do.	5 do.	2nd do.	2 do.
3rd do.	4 do.	3rd do.	1 do.

Rule XV Children shall not be admitted into the School under the age of seven years, nor shall any be admitted without procuring a Ticket signed by one of the Members of the Visiting Committee, stating the name and age of the Child, and also the occupation and residence of the Parents.

Rule XVI The Parents or Friends of each Child are to send with it one penny every Monday Morning, and one half-penny more for each additional Child they may have in the School, the money thus sent to be paid into the hands of the Master or Mistress. All arrears are to be paid up on the Monday preceding each Monthly Meeting of the Committee; otherwise the Master and Mistress are to give notice to the Parents of all such Children, as are then in arrear, to attend the Meeting of the Committee; and if no satisfactory reason then be assigned for their failure in the required weekly payments, their Children will be excluded from the School.

Rule XVII Every Boy or Girl who shall have obtained temporary leave of absence except it be on account of sickness, shall be required to attend the Sunday School.

Rule XVIII The Vacations in this School, are a fortnight at Christmas, a fortnight in the Turf season, and a fortnight in Harvest. The other Holidays are Easter Monday and Tuesday, Whit-Monday and Tuesday, and such other days as the Patroness may direct.

SELECT BIBLIOGRAPHY

Much the best history of the land of Cartmel is that in the *Victoria County History of Lancaster* (1914) vol. 8 pp. 254-85; vol. 2 of the same work has a useful article on Cartmel Priory but local mills and schools do not get adequate treatment here. Useful snippets of information on our area are to be had from the older county histories and the early trade directories and guide-books, but these are not always accurate. J. Stockdale, *Annals of Cartmel* (Ulverston 1872 recently reprinted) is massive but badly planned; it is of fundamental importance through the amount of documents it prints and valuable personal recollections included, though on pre-Tudor centuries it is not always accurate.

T. W. Potter, *Romans in North West England* (Kendal 1979) has inevitably little to say on Cartmel, but is important for its picture of the general background. For the rest of the pre-Conquest period place-names are our only sizeable source. E. Ekwall, *Place-names of Lancashire* (Manchester 1922) is rather sketchy compared with the English Place-name Society volumes on Cumberland (3 vols. ed. A. M. Armstrong C.U.P. 1950-2) and Westmorland (2 vols. ed. A. H. Smith 1967).

From post-Conquest times onwards the chief secondary sources are the *Victoria County History* and the volumes of the *Transactions of the Cumberland and Westmorland Antiquarian and Archaeological Society*, whose Old Series covers the period 1866-1900 and New Series that from 1900 to the present day. For church history C. M. L. Bouch, *Prelates and People of the Lake Counties*, is a good study of all Cumbria from 1133 to recent times, and *The Rural Deanery of Cartmel* (1892) ed. R. H. Kirkby and others is a useful little work. More specialised are C. Haigh's *The Last Days of the Lancashire Monasteries* ... (1969) and his *Reform and Resistance in Tudor Lancashire* (1975) both published by the Chetham Society. The bells of Cartmel are studied in "The Church Bells of Lancashire: North Lonsdale" (*Transactions of the Lancs. and Cheshire Antiq. Soc.*, xl, 1922-3 and the books in "The ancient library of Cartmel Priory Church (2nd. Edn. Durham 1959) by S. Taylor and D. Ramage. For local railway history see W. McG. Gradon *The Furness Railway, its rise and development 1846-1923* (1946). *Early Railway History in Furness* (Kendal 1951) by J. Melville and J. Hobbs. Of the flood of guide books to the area *Sketches of Grange and the Neighbourhood* (1850) is excellent and has attractive illustrations. *The Cartmel and Lower Holker Almanac* 1888 is an entertaining private venture which contains local notes. *An Armorial for Westmorland and Lonsdale* (Kendal 1975) by R. S. Boumphrey, C. R. Hudleston and J. Hughes is a useful guide to local armigerous families. The Cartmel Enclosure Act is the subject of an unpublished thesis.

The Lancashire Parish Register Society has published the Cartmel registers from 1559-1723 in two volumes. The reprint of the government survey "The Public

Charities of the Hundred of Lonsdale North of the Sands" (Ulverston 1852) contains much interesting Cartmel information. The early archives of the Holker Hall estates are deposited in the County Record Office at Preston; a catalogue of them has been published. More local material exists in the Record Offices at Kendal and Barrow-in-Furness.

INDEX

(Buildings of the Priory and Contents of the Church are indexed under CARTMEL PRIORY.)

Abbot Hall, Kents Bank, 24, 54, 67-8
agriculture, 63f.
Allithwaite, 6, 56, 67-72
Andrew St., Moor, 73
Angles, 5-6
Armstrong, Rev. J., 25-6
Augustine, Rule of, 12
Austin Canons, 11-12
Ay, 55
Aynsome, 15, 85
    Mill, 55
axes, prehistoric, 3

Backbarrow Cotton Mill, 58-9
Ballymaden, 15
Ballysax, 15
Barngarth, 18, 19, 39
Barrow-in-Furness, 51
Beetham, 15
Big Mill, Cark, 57-8
Bigland, 75
    Hall, 75
Birkby, 3, 71
Boarbank Hall, 70-1
Board of Agriculture, 63n.
Bolton priory, 54
Bolton le Sands, 14, 44
Borrowdale, 48
Bottomley, Gordon, 39
Bowness church, glass in, 16, 22, 87-8
Braddyll, Colonel, 46
Bradenstoke priory, 10
Brigge, Thomas, 22, 23
Briggs, J., 5
Briggs, Rowland, 31
British Museum, 3n.
brobs, 44
Broughton, Sir Thomas, 14
Broughton (in Cartmel), 4, 6, 15, 24, 72-4
Broughton church, 74
    Grange, 74

Broughton church,
    Hall, 74
    House, 74
    Lodge, 74
Burlington, Earl of, 79, 80

Canon Winder Hall, 90
Cark, 7, 47, 51, 52, 56f., 75-8
    Hall, 55, 76-7
    House, 78
    Mills, 78
    Shaws, 54
Carlisle, bishopric of, 8
Cart Lane, 42, 49
Carter, the, 42-3
Cartmel cloth, 61
    Enclosure Act (1796), 63-5
Cartmel, land of, 1f., 7, 10, 11, 13, 15, 54-5, 81
    Market place, 82
    name of, 7
    school, 84
    village, 82-5
Cartmel Priory, land of, 1, 4, 8, 10, 13, 48, 51, 81
    architecture 16, 22
    Austin canon, effigy of, 37
    canons of, 16, 22
    bread charity, 30
    candelabra, 39
    chancel, 32-5
    choir screen, 33
    choir stalls, 33
    churchyard, 29
    coat of arms of, 4
    conventual buildings, 13, 39-40
    Cromwell door, 29
    crossing, 39
    east window, 32, 38, Fig. 3
    foundation of, 10-12
    foundation charters, 97-8
    gatehouse, 40
    Harrington tomb, 35-6
    library, 26, 32
    misericords, 33-5
    nave, 30-1
    north transept, 31-2

Cartmel Priory, land of,
  officials, 16
  organ, 25, 35
  Piper Choir, 31
  plan of church, 28
  porch, 29
  possessions of, 14-16
  Rod of Jesse, 37
  south transept, 37-8
  stained glass, 32, 34
  stocks at, 29
  Suppression of, 21-4
  Thornburgh memorial, 39
  Town Choir, 35-7
  umbrella, ancient, 32
  vestry, 25, 32
  Walton, William, tomb of, 33
Cartmel, village of, 82-5
Cartmel Fell, 22, 85-8
  church, 22, 50, 85-7
Castle Head, 3-4, 55, 95
Causeway End, 14
Cavendish, Lady Frederick, 80, 89
  Lord Frederick, 30, 80
  Lord George, 49, 63
Cavendish Arms, 46
Chaloner, Dr. W. K., 57
Chapel Island, 46, 47, 50
Charcoal, 60n.
Chester, bishopric of, 24, 39
Clarke, J., 48
clocks, local, 62-3
coaches, 49
cockles, 62
cock-fighting, 85
Conishead priory, 7, 10, 15, 44, 46
Coniston, 52
Conquest, Norman, 7
corn mills, 55-9
cotton mill, 57-8
Cox, David, 45
Court, Thomas, mariner, 62
Cromwellians, 25, 29, 70, 84
Curwen, Robert, 76

Dacre, Lady Joan, 36
Devonshire, 7th Duke of, 79-80
dialect, local, 7
Dicconson family, 31, 69
Dickins, Prof. B., 4
Dickinson, John, Clockmaker, 63
Dissolution of the Monasteries, 21f.
Domesday Book, 7-8, 9

Egg Pudding Stone, 73
Eggerslack, 4, 91-2
enclosures, 63f.
Enclosures of the Commons, 64-5

Field, William, 4
fire brigade, Holker, 81
fishing, Flookburgh, 62
Flodden, battle of, 69
Flookburgh, 7, 13, 24, 26, 44, 45, 49, 62, 88-90
  charter, 99
  church, 88-9
  fire, 91
  market, 89, 98
  plague, 90-1
  regalia, 89
foreigner, French, 100
Fox, George, 26
Frith Hall, 78
Furness abbey, 10, 25, 67
  Michael de, 46
  Railway, 51f.
furniture, local, 62

Gatehouse, priory, 40
Gibson, William, mathematician, 101-3
Grange-over-Sands, 7, 15, 51, 54, 91-3
  churches, 93
  Hall, 93
  harbour, 91-3
  Hotel, 93
  railway, 93
Green, William, 44, 48
gunpowder mill, 59-60

Haigh, Dr. C., 21
Hampsfield, 6
  Hall, 72-3
Harrington, Lord, John, 18, 35-6, 37, 68, 71
  Lord William, 20, 68
  tomb, 35-6
Haverthwaite, 6
Hazelslack tower, 69
Helton tarn, 15
Hemans, Mrs. F., 47
Hest Bank, 41, 44
Heversham, 5
Hill Mill, 55
Holker, 15, 78-81
Holker Bank, 2
  Charity School, 104-6
  Hall, 52, 54, 63, 77, 78-81
Holme Island, 6, 43n.

INDEX

Holy Cross, relic, of, 22
Holy Well, Humphrey Head, 71-2
Hospice, the, 73
Humphrey Head, 6, 14, 50, 71-2
hundreds, 8

Ireland, 14-15
iron trade, 54-5

John, King, 10, 11, 14, 43

Keir, river, 42
Kendal, cloth, 60-1
    Tommy, 52
Kents Bank, 51, 54, 68
Kilrush, 15
King, Mr. D., 27
Kirkby Cartmel, 7, 8
Kirkby Ireleth, 51
Kirkhead, 14
    cave, 2
    chapel, 5, 11
    tower, 68
Knipe, family of, 74

"Lady of the Lake", 52
Lambert, Miss, 67, 70, 72
Lancaster, 4, 5, 8
Lanercost chronicle, 13
Last Wolf, The, 71
Law, Bp. Edmund, 82
Leven, 44, 48, 53n., 55
Lindale (in Cartmel), 3, 4, 7, 24, 93-4
    chapel, 94-5
    and church, 94-5
Little Mill, Cark, 56
lock-up, Cartmel, 82
Lonsdale, 1, 8, 10, 12
Lonsdale Magazine, 41, 42, 44-5, 59, 79, 85
Lourdes, Order of Our Lady of, 71
Low Wood mill, 61
Lowther, family of, 79
    Sir James, 49
    Sir William, 37

Machell, James, 54
Marshall, Mrs. Margaret, 39
    William, Earl of Pembroke, 10, 11
mills, 55f.
misericords, 33-5
Myers, William, 31

Newton, 6, 7, 8, 74-5
Northumbria, 5

Organ, 25, 28, 35
Outerthwaite, 6

pack horse tracks, 49
paper mill, 56
Pennington, 7
Pickering, Thomas, 76
Piel Castle, 10, 13
Pilgrimage of Grace, 23-4
Pit Farm, 54
poor, alms to, 15
pound, 74
Preston, family of, 24, 79
    George, 25, 30
    Thomas, 26, 54
Priest Lane, 39
Priory Close, 82

Quakers, 26
quarry, limestone, 63
Quarry Flat, 64

Railways, 50f.
Ransome, Arthur, 84-5
Raven Winder, 6
Rawlinson, family, 76
    Christopher, 76-7
Reckitts Ltd., 59
Remington, Rev. T., 26-7, 73
roads, 47f.
Robinson, William, 25
Rollinson, Dr. W., 63n.
Romans, 3-5
Rosthwaite, 6, 77
runes, 6-7

Sandgate, 45-6
Sands, route over, 15f.
Scottish raids, 13
shipping, 61-2
Silverdale, 14, 15
Simnel, Lambert, 13-14, 69
Spenser, *Faerie Queen*, 26
St. Andrew Moor, 73
Stanley, Thomas, Earl of Derby, 69
Staveley, 24, 75
    chapel, 75
Stephenson, George, 50
Stockdale, J., 47, 49, 57, 64

Taxation of Pope Nicholas, 15
Taylor, Canon S., 7
Taylor, William, 29
Tenter Bank, Cark, 61
Thornburgh, Michael, 23
    Ethelred, 24
    Sir William, 73
Thorpensty, 6
Thurston Water, 6
Tide table (1822), 41
Town Choir, 18-19
travel, local, 41-53
Turner, J. M. W., 45
Turnpikes, 48

Ulverston, 49
Ulverston and Lancaster Rly., 51-2

Valor Ecclesiasticus, 46
Vasconcellas, Josephina da, 30
Vikings, 6-7
visitation of Cartmel priory, 12

Walton, 2, 3, 4, 8, 55, 85
Waytholme, 6
Wesley, John, 26, 46
West, Thomas, 46
Whittington Church, 15
Wilkinson, Isaac, 6, 54, 95
    John, 33-42, 54, 95
Willan, Brian, 22, 23, 24
William, St., of York, 32
William de Walton, prior, 33
    prior of Cartmel, 88
Wilson House, 54
Winder, 64
    Moor, 3, 90
Windermere, 6 *see also* Bowness
wolf, the "last", 71
wool trade, 60-1
Wordsworth, William, 47
Wraysholme, 6, 31, 42, 44, 63, 68-70

York, archbishops of, 12, 13, 15, 32
    minster, 19, 32
Young, Arthur, 47